YAHOO! TO THE MAX

YAHOO! TO THE MAX

An Extreme Searcher Guide

Randolph Hock

CyberAge Books

Information Today, Inc.
Medford, New Jersey

Yahoo! to the Max
An Extreme Searcher Guide

Library of Congress Cataloging-in-Publication Data

Hock, Randolph, 1944-
 Yahoo! to the max : an extreme searcher guide / Randolph Hock ; foreword by Mary Ellen Bates.
   p. cm.
 Includes index.
  ISBN: 0-910965-69-2
1. Yahoo! (Computer file) 2. Web search engines.   I. Title
 ZA4234 Y33H63 2005
 025.04--dc22

                 2005007371

Printed and bound in the United States of America.

President and CEO: Thomas H. Hogan, Sr.
Editor-in-Chief and Publisher: John B. Bryans
Managing Editor: Amy M. Holmes
Project Editor: Reva Basch
VP Graphics and Production: M. Heide Dengler
Book Designer: Kara Mia Jalkowski
Cover Designer: Shelley Szajner
Proofreader: Pat Hadley-Miller
Indexer: Sharon Hughes

DEDICATION

To Pamela, Matthew, Stephen, and Elizabeth

CONTENTS

FiGURES

TABLES

FOREWORD

I have known Ran Hock for years, first merely by reputation as "that guy who really knows how to search Dialog." Since then, I have been fortunate enough to hear his talks at many Information Today conferences, and I have read his Extreme Searcher books. Now he has moved from Extreme to The Max; I wonder if this suggests that, while you don't have to be extreme to get the most from a search engine, you do have to move beyond the basics. And, as someone who wrote a couple of books in Information Today's Super Searchers series, I am humbled to realize that "Super" isn't all that hot, when you can take it to the max!

I was particularly happy to see that Ran's latest book focuses on Yahoo!. Over the past year or so, I have noticed that I use, well, that other search engine (you know, the one that starts with "G" and ends with "e" and rhymes with oogle) much less frequently than I used to. Yahoo! has rolled out a lot of cool features, tools, and resources, and whenever something new comes out, I know that it will be well thought out, well-integrated into the rest of Yahoo!'s services, and worth taking on a test drive.

When I first started using, and teaching others to use, the Internet back in the mid-1990s, our favorite resource by far was the venerable Yahoo! directory. Built by humans—often librarians, no less—and organized into sensible categories, it felt like a respite from what often seemed like the World Wild Web.

As I expected, Ran has done his usual excellent job at explaining the wide range of features available on Yahoo! in Yahoo! to the Max. I shouldn't be surprised by now, having read his other Extreme Searcher books, but I still marvel that I've even learned new things about the Yahoo! features I use all the time.

For example, I always wondered what those @ signs were at the end of some Yahoo! Directory categories. A-ha! They're indications that the category is actually being cross-referenced from another area within the directory.

So I have just learned that I should watch for those @'s, knowing that they will help me expand my research into areas I might not have thought of otherwise.

I have been using the Calendar function within My Yahoo! for a couple of years to coordinate my schedule with two colleagues. But I had no idea that I could print out a list of our respective schedules, sorted by speaking gigs, vacations, consulting travel, and so on. Cool!

Yahoo! Groups is one of my favorite and—until now, I had thought, secret—tool for research on obscure topics. I find it to be a really useful way of tapping into the knowledge base of people who follow a specific topic—emergency radio frequencies, women's hiking trips in the Rocky Mountains, new trends in data visualization—but I never realized that I could monitor the messages from Yahoo! Groups through my RSS reader. I have already added several Yahoo! Groups to my unfortunately too-quickly expanding list of RSS feeds. Thanks, Ran, for contributing to my information overload!

While I point people to Yahoo! Finance for stock quotes and related company information, I didn't realize that it also offered online quizzes to test readers' financial savvy. And as a far-too-frequent business traveler, I had no idea how much information I could find in the Travel Guides. My next trip to Australia will be that much simpler, now that I see how much I can organize ahead of time through Yahoo!.

Once again, Ran has written a tremendously useful book, my copy of which, I fear, will soon become dog-eared, marked up, and littered with sticky-notes. I suggest that you do not share your copy of this book with someone else, as you will probably never get it back.

Mary Ellen Bates
Bates Information Services, Inc.
Boulder, Colorado
February 2005

ACKNOWLEDGMENTS

Though it may seem simple to readers, I find the Acknowledgments page to be one of the more difficult parts of the book to write. As the very last thing to be submitted, writing this page means that my part of the job is really over. The writer's equivalent of postpartum blues threaten to set in. On the other hand, it is a time for celebration, jubilation, and if I were so inclined, maybe inebriation. More relevant though, writing acknowledgments is humbling and challenging. It is one of the (actually many) times when the author humbly realizes that his work really is just a part of the whole. It is challenging to write because one knows that for some of the people to be thanked, the adequate phrases will just not come, and that there are people who should be thanked who will be left out, some of whom aren't even personally known to the author. In any case, the following are some of the people to whom I owe thanks.

John Bryans, Editor-in-Chief and Publisher of the Books Division at Information Today, Inc., goes above and beyond the call of duty in being involved with and showing support for each of my books, from when I first broach the idea of the book through its entire life. In addition to his expertise and knowledge, he provides frequent doses of both enthusiasm and reality, from the biggest issues to the smallest. I am deeply grateful to John for his knowledge, support, and friendship.

I feel very lucky that Amy Holmes, Managing Editor of Information Today's Books Division, is handling the editorial side of this project. I am extremely grateful not just for her expertise, input, and astute observations, but also for the extraordinary flexibility she has shown. There were many times when she could have legitimately said, "No, that involves too much work at my end," but instead, she cheerfully said, "Yes." Amy is an author's dream!

I am also much indebted to Reva Basch, Project Editor. I am very fortunate that John chose her for the job. I suspect that it is rare that an author is provided with an editor who has Reva's combination of writing skills and subject expertise. Because of this combination and her care and diligence, there are a lot of places in the book that are now much easier for the reader to understand.

I also wish to thank Mary Ellen Bates, colleague and friend, who was kind enough to write the Foreword. She is proof of the adage, "If you want to get something done, and done right, ask a busy person." I am truly grateful that she was willing to take time out from her very busy work and travel schedule to do this.

There are a number of other people at Information Today to whom I also owe thanks. These include Heide Dengler and her staff, including the book's designer, Kara Jalkowski, and the cover designer, Shelley Szajner. I hope that readers will be as impressed as I am with what they have delivered. Once again, I thank Tom Hogan Sr. for the existence of Information Today and for his enthusiasm for my books. I am always grateful to Heather Rudolph, Marketing Manager, for being there to get innumerable things done on the marketing side. Thanks also to Tom Hogan Jr., for his broader role in the marketing of the book.

Finally, I thank the readers of my previous books and the attendees of my workshops for their continued support, encouragement, and inspiration.

PREFACE

The reason I wrote this book (besides helping to provide lunch money for my kids) is that I am very impressed with Yahoo!. Yahoo! does more for me than any other Web site.

At first, I spent relatively little time with Yahoo! in my Internet workshops. However, the more I used it, especially after I made "My Yahoo!" my start page, the more I began to discover its thousands of valuable nooks and crannies. Then, in 2004, Yahoo! switched its emphasis from "directory" to "search." The same year, Yahoo! developed a Web search database of its own that is very competitive with Google's. At that point, it was apparent that serious searchers—"extreme" searchers, "power" searchers, call them what you will—could use a book aimed at helping them get the most from Yahoo!.

Yahoo! is one of the most powerful and content-rich sites on the Internet. Its features and excellent content are very well integrated. For instance, you can immerse yourself in news on Yahoo!'s News page, but you can also select particular news categories that will appear on your "My Yahoo!" page. Not only that, you can have News Alerts sent to you via e-mail or Yahoo!'s Instant Messaging service. Yahoo! fits the pieces together very nicely, and in doing so makes the whole significantly greater than the sum of its parts.

The downside of such a rich site is that, given Yahoo!'s range of content, the interconnections among different content areas, and the variety of ways to get at that content, it's not easy to gain a quick grasp on what the site can do and what you can do with it.

This book is aimed at helping you easily identify and use the parts of Yahoo! that are relevant to you. It is arranged so that you can readily spot and skip over the sections that are obviously of no interest. Of course, since I spent hundreds of hours slaving over a hot keyboard to carefully craft every word in the book, I hope you won't skip a single one. I would like to think that every sentence I have written here has a chance of improving your life and the well-being of humanity. (Humility is just one of my many strong points.) More realistically, I hope you will at least skim all sections of the book. Some Yahoo! features that might sound uninteresting on the surface could prove useful to you in ways you didn't expect.

As much as I like Yahoo!, I will quickly admit that it's not perfect. As with just about any very large site, some of its features don't work perfectly 100 percent of the time. Considering the number of Yahoo!'s offerings and the breadth of its content, such failings are relatively rare. For the most part I have only good things to say about Yahoo!. Occasionally I will mention a weakness, but the good things are what's valuable and where the emphasis will lie. Sometimes, you'll find I get almost effusive, because I really am that enthusiastic about some of Yahoo!'s offerings. But I try at least for a modicum of objectivity. For example, the reason I think that My Yahoo! is the Web's best general portal is because I have rigorously compared it to the others, even if the actual comparisons don't appear in this book.

How much detail to present was a particularly challenging issue. I have tried to mention everything that I think a power user should know about. I have made an effort to include information that should be useful in quickly getting to know your way around and learning how to do what you'll probably want to do. I have gone into great detail in describing some Yahoo! pages, functions, and features; I've pointed out virtually every item on the page if I think they're useful and might be missed by someone visiting there for the first time. In other places, I've purposely left out items that I think are trivial, obvious, or advertisements. I have used a "click here, then click there" approach only where I think it would be useful. Where a potential application of a feature is not obvious, I have tried to point out why you might want to use it.

This is not intended to be the definitive, "everything anyone might ever want to know about Yahoo!" book. It *is* intended to guide the serious, "extreme" user in getting the most from Yahoo!.

One last word: Be aware that sites like Yahoo! are constantly being refined, updated, and reorganized, and that the location, or even presence, of a link or other content may change. If something is not where I say it is, just look elsewhere on the page, or use Yahoo!'s own search function to locate the feature or content you want.

I hope that this book will indeed help you "get the max" from Yahoo!.

ABOUT THE EXTREME SEARCHER'S WEB PAGE

www.extremesearcher.com

Yahoo! is, fortunately, constantly changing—adding content, occasionally dropping content, rearranging things, and otherwise changing its design. To help you keep aware of changes that have occurred since the publication of this book, a Web page for *Yahoo! to the Max* is provided by the author. It is part of The Extreme Searcher's Web Page and is available at www.extremesearcher.com.

Enjoy your visit there and please send any feedback by e-mail to ran@extremesearcher.com.

Disclaimer:
Neither publisher nor author make any claim as to the results that may be obtained through the use of *The Extreme Searcher's Web Page* or of any of the Internet resources it references or links to. Neither publisher nor author will be held liable for any results, or lack thereof, obtained by the use of this page or any of its links; for any third-party charges; or for any hardware, software, or other problems that may occur as a result of using it. *The Extreme Searcher's Web Page* is subject to change or discontinuation without notice at the discretion of the publisher and author.

CHAPTER 1

Yahoo!'s Home Page: An Overview of Yahoo!

If you were on the proverbial desert island and could only have access to one Web site, you might want to consider Yahoo!. Yes, I know that you might reject the idea, preferring instead something more obviously practical like a survival site, a boat-building site, or a Jimmy Buffet site. But consider Yahoo! anyway.

Wherever you find yourself, if you take the Web seriously you *have* to be familiar with Yahoo!. Knowing the site even moderately well can increase your ease, efficiency, and effectiveness in accessing not only content, but the full potential of the Internet. Yahoo! has a unique "personality." It presents some apparent contradictions: It's simple to use, but it's also complex; it's straightforward, but it also contains many hidden resources and tools. Yahoo! is a site for novice Internet users, as well as the most sophisticated.

Yahoo! is indeed easy to use, but it is not easy to discover all of the features that exist *for* you to use. "Getting the max" from Yahoo! depends on identifying tools and content that are potentially useful, and then exploring what they can do for you personally. As you explore, you will discover multiple dimensions to Yahoo!'s strength. Yahoo! presents its tremendous range of content not just as a collection of pieces, but integrated in various helpful ways that make the whole of Yahoo! greater than the sum of its parts. On top of that, Yahoo! is a leader in "personalization." It lets *you* determine what content is most valuable, and presents you with what you need when you need it, rather than just delivering what it's determined the "average" user's needs.

A Bit of Yahoo! History

Before delving into what Yahoo! can do for you, it's appropriate to say a few words about how it came about in the first place. Yahoo! was started in 1994 by two Stanford University graduate students, David Filo and Jerry Yang. Recognizing that the number of useful Web sites was increasing rapidly and that keeping them straight was a challenge, they developed a collection of selected sites arranged in categories—a Web directory, in effect—and made it available to others. Its popularity grew rapidly and in 1996 the company went public. By then, it had already become more than a directory, with an increasing number of "portal" features such as links to stock quotes, Yellow Pages, maps, and so on. It had also begun to provide search access to many more sites beyond those listed in the directory—sites found by crawling the Web, and neither categorized nor individually selected by human beings.

The number of resources, partnerships, and services had also continued to increase vigorously. By 2004, the directory function had taken a back seat to the portal and search functions. Yahoo! had developed its own "crawled" database, instead of relying on one provided by others, and its directory was no longer the centerpiece of the site. In August 2004 Yahoo! unveiled a home page that no longer even prominently displayed the directory. Search and portal offerings are now where it's at. At present Yahoo! has more than 2,000 partners that help provide the largest collection of wide-ranging services, such as research, news, travel, shopping, and entertainment, available through any Web portal.

Exploring with Yahoo!

As with many other Web sites, the key to using Yahoo! is to *explore*. When explorers set out to investigate new territory, having a native guide to take them at least part of the way often determines the success of their expedition. I hope this book will act as such a guide. I also hope it will provide, like a human guide, some insights and suggestions that will continue to serve you as you explore on your own, and as Yahoo! continues to change.

Along those lines, here's one suggestion that may be familiar if you have read other books in the "Extreme Searcher" series: When you really want to know a site, *click everywhere*! The catch is that few people have the time to really do that. Theoretically, at least, clicking everywhere you possibly can on Yahoo!'s home page (www.yahoo.com) will acquaint you with Yahoo!'s main offerings and give you a good start in understanding what it's all about. You'll also come to appreciate the degree to which its home page can serve as a gateway to the rest of Yahoo! (see Figure 1.1).

In this chapter you will find a description of the features and options on the home page, as well as some general information about procedures such as signing up and managing your Yahoo!

Figure 1.1 Yahoo! Home Page

account, privacy and anonymity issues, and some pan-Yahoo! features such as Yahoo!'s Companion Toolbar. Most of the features described below are discussed in detail in later chapters. Some, including My Yahoo!, Search, Groups, and News, have chapters of their own. Even if you just skim the brief descriptions that follow, be sure to read the sections at the end of this chapter on Yahoo! accounts, the Yahoo! Toolbar, etc.

YAHOO! HOME PAGE CONTENTS

Yahoo!'s front page includes more than 50 links to Yahoo! content and services (plus, of course, a few ads). It serves, as a home page should, as a gateway to the overall contents of the Yahoo! site. This section takes a quick look at what you will find behind those links. Though items move around now and then, and names occasionally change, in general the links on the Yahoo! main page are arranged in the following areas:

- **Links to Yahoo!'s most central services,** such as My Yahoo!, Mail, Search, Finance, Travel, and Messenger – These features, showcased at the top of the page, will vary depending on which ones Yahoo! is currently promoting and if you are signed in, an edit link allows you to select which are shown.
- **The Yahoo! Web search box** and links to its other large searchable databases, such as Images, Directory, Local, News, and Products, and to the Advanced Search page.
- **The Yahoo! Services Directory** – This is the doorway to the entire range of services provided by Yahoo!. Most services are listed here, but look for a link labeled something like See All Yahoo! Services or Even More Yahoo!; this will lead to a more definitive list.
- **In the News** – Provides selection of the day's headlines, with links to the full Yahoo! News section.
- **Weather** – Access to your local (U.S.-only) weather conditions.
- **Marketplace** – Features selected ads.

- **Entertainment** – Offers links to featured entertainment content.
- **Links to Yahoo!'s fee-based Premium and Business services.**
- **Local Yahoo!s/World Yahoo!s/Yahoo! International** – Though the names vary, these are links to assorted country-specific, U.S. city-specific, and language-specific versions of Yahoo!.
- **More Yahoo! Services** – Consists of links to Yahoo! services and sections that may not have made it to the top of the site.
- **Web Directory** – Depending on how far Yahoo! has gone in de-emphasizing its role as a Web directory provider, you may have to look fairly carefully to find this one. The Directory is what used to be the core of Yahoo!, the categories that lead you deeper into Yahoo!'s browsable collection of selected Web sites.
- **Links to Terms of Service**, other Yahoo! policies, etc.

A QUICK LOOK AT INDIVIDUAL HOME PAGE LINKS

This section describes the various links in each of the areas of the Yahoo! main page that were just discussed. A look at each of these will not only provide a general orientation and sense of where they will lead you, but will help you quickly identify which of Yahoo!'s offerings are likely to be of most interest. Since the locations of some of these links tend to change, they are listed alphabetically. (If you don't find one of these items on the home page, check the More Yahoo! or Even More Yahoo! links.)

Addresses – Store addresses, phone numbers, and related information for use in conjunction with your Yahoo! Mail, Groups, and Calendar, or just for quick lookup. For the latter, it can be your "traveling" address book. See Chapter 3, My Yahoo!: The Best General Portal on the Web, for more about the Address Book.

Astrology – Get your daily horoscope and participate in groups, message boards, and chatrooms about astrology.

Auctions – Bid on and buy items for sale by individuals and companies, and sell your own items as well. See Chapter 7, Buying and Selling Through Yahoo!, for more about Yahoo! Auctions.

Autos – Research new and used cars and car prices, and buy and sell cars. Additional resources provide information on auto financing and insurance.

Briefcase – Store files on Yahoo! and access them from anywhere in the world. The Yahoo! Briefcase gives you 30 MB of free storage space. Briefcase also lets you share files with others. See Chapter 3 for more about Yahoo! Briefcase.

Calendar – Enter events and tasks into a personal online calendar. You can also request e-mail reminders, list and print calendar pages and events in a variety of ways, share your calendar (or just the entries that you choose) with others, synchronize your Yahoo! Calendar with other programs and devices such as Outlook and Palm OS handhelds, and lots more. For details on the calendar, see Chapter 3.

Chat – Talk online with people around the world—friends, acquaintances, and strangers. Chat rooms may appeal to you, but I think most people will get less out of them than they might expect. Yahoo! provides much better alternatives for communicating with others. See Chapter 6, Yahoo!: The Great Communicator, for details.

Classifieds – Buy and sell items as you would from newspaper classified ads, but with added search capabilities and greater interaction. The Classifieds cover not just merchandise, but job postings (Yahoo! HotJobs), real estate, rentals, tickets, and more. See Chapter 7 for more details.

Finance – Gain access to a very broad range of statistics, advice, news, background, tools, and services related to finance and investing. Outstanding among these is the information on markets, particularly the personal portfolios you can set up. Chapter 8 is devoted to Yahoo! Finance.

Games – Play games by yourself, or with others on the Internet. Yahoo! Games offers games you can download and play offline, as well as leagues and tournaments you can join. At any given time, you're likely to find more than 100,000 players online. All games are Java-based. In addition to free games, Yahoo! offers Premium games for a fee. These include the games you see under Games All-Stars, Games Downloads, and Games on Demand. If you'd like to explore Yahoo! Games, start by downloading one of the Arcade games. Be aware, though, that you generally get just a "demo" version that you can only play for a limited period or a limited number of times before having to purchase it. For multiplayer games, Yahoo! supplies detailed descriptions, rules of play, and instructions.

GeoCities – Get a site up and going in as little as a few minutes, even without any experience in building Web pages. In the early 2000s, many services around the Web specialized in providing free Web sites. One of the relatively few survivors is GeoCities, which is now owned by Yahoo!. It survived because it was and is one of the best. See Chapter 6 for more information about GeoCities.

Greetings – For an annual subscription fee, send e-mail greeting cards to anyone with an e-mail address. Some are available for free.

Groups – Participate in group discussions on thousands of topics and easily and quickly create your own group on any topic you wish. These groups provide a forum that is immensely better than Chat. With Groups you can have moderated or unmoderated discussions, share files and photos, maintain databases and a group calendar, conduct polls, and much more. Yahoo! Groups is one of the services that users (and nonusers) of Yahoo! should get to know. See Chapter 4 for a detailed look at Yahoo! Groups.

Health – Search a broad range of information on various diseases and conditions. Also included is a medical encyclopedia, a drug guide, health news, expert advice, and information on clinical trials. For more details on Yahoo!'s Health section, see Chapter 9, Other Seriously Useful Yahoo! Stuff.

HotJobs – Search for jobs by keyword or city and state, as well as post your own availability. You can create a resume online, run saved job searches ("agents") you have set up, and see the "Hottest Jobs" in your area.

Kids – Access Yahooligans!, The Web Guide for Kids, a well-respected safe place for children online. Kids can play games, tap into homework resources, and find their way to selected Web sites via the Yahooligans! directory, and much more. Chapter 9 discusses Yahooligans! in more detail.

Local Yahoo!s/International Yahoos! – Search country- or region-specific versions of Yahoo! The default version of Yahoo! at yahoo.com has a significantly "U.S.-centric" orientation. Many services on Yahoo!'s main page, such as People Search, Yellow Pages, TV and Movies, serve up just U.S. (and in some cases Canadian) information. To make Yahoo! more relevant to non-U.S. users, Yahoo! has produced more than two-dozen country- or region-specific versions that provide more localized content. You should consider using one of these versions if you are located outside the U.S., and even when searching for information *about* any of those regions. Also, take advantage of the fact that many individual sections of Yahoo!, such as Travel and Finance, include links to country-specific Yahoo! sites for that topic. Chapter 9 discusses Local Yahoo!s in more detail.

Mail – Sign up for Yahoo! e-mail. Even if you have another e-mail account at work or elsewhere, it's worth signing up for Yahoo!'s robust Web-accessible e-mail service. In addition to the usual e-mail functions, Yahoo! Mail provides convenient and unique tie-ins to other Yahoo! services, such as News and Finance. Chapter 6 discusses Yahoo! Mail.

Make Yahoo! your home page – Make yahoo.com the start page for your browser. But consider using a My Yahoo! page (see below) instead. My Yahoo! allows you to personalize your content and your view of Yahoo!, and will probably be a much more relevant and useful start page.

Maps – Get maps and driving directions for destinations in the U.S. or Canada. Maps can be personalized with your choice of locations such as local restaurants, banks, recreation spots, and transportation. Read more about maps in Chapter 9.

Messenger – Communicate with friends and acquaintances who are online when you are using Yahoo!'s Instant Messaging (IM). Messenger offers real-time communication, and is also integrated with Yahoo! services such as News Alerts, Web searching, and file transfer. For details on Messenger, see Chapter 6.

Mobile – Learn how to access many of Yahoo!'s services via mobile devices such as cell phones and PDAs. These include Messenger, Mail, News and other Alerts, games, photos, and even Web searching. Yahoo! Mobile is discussed in Chapter 9.

More Yahoo! – Get a quick and simplified glimpse of what Yahoo! offers. More Yahoo! is your gateway to all, or nearly all, of Yahoo!'s sections and services. It includes links to features that didn't make it to the home page, such as the Yahoo! Member Directory, Family Accounts, Pets, Postal Center (ZIP code lookup and package tracking), lottery results, and fantasy sports. You'll also find links to business and marketing services such as Web hosting, enhanced listings on search results pages, and Yahoo! Express, which guarantees priority evaluation of your site for the Yahoo! directory. More Yahoo! offers links to other premium offerings as well, including Yahoo! phone cards, DSL and dial-up ISP services, and searching by phone and voice mail.

Movies – Find reviews, showtimes, trailers and clips, biographies, filmographies, news, and more—about new movies and old, what's in the theaters, and what's on DVD and video. A search box provides easy access to movie information. See Chapter 3 for details.

Music – Read about and listen to your favorite musicians. The "LAUNCH - Music on Yahoo!" section features information, interviews, and videos about musicians, groups, and recordings. LAUNCH also provides customizable Internet radio channels for many musical genres; you can listen to the music you like while exploring the rest of Yahoo!'s offerings. See Chapter 9 for more on LAUNCH.

My Yahoo! – Personalize your home page with your own selection of Yahoo! content, features, and services. For many people, My

Yahoo! may be the most important part of the site. The Personalize link is a constant reminder that the utility of Yahoo! is tremendously enhanced by your ability to select just the items and categories of information that interest you, and to organize it the way you want. Since My Yahoo! is so powerful and useful, it will come as no surprise that Chapter 3, which is devoted to this aspect of Yahoo!, is the longest chapter in this book.

News – Access up-to-date news on Yahoo! News, one of the most robust news sites on the Web. Its front page shows major headlines and includes news from more than 7,000 sources, in 35 languages. Yahoo! News is extensively searchable and browsable. In addition, you can set up news alerts to be delivered via e-mail or Messenger, and take advantage of other features as well. Chapter 5 covers Yahoo! News.

People Search – Search Yahoo!'s "white pages" for postal and e-mail addresses. For more on People Search, see Chapter 9.

Personals – Learn about Yahoo!'s online dating service. You're on your own with this one.

Photos – Store your digital photos on Yahoo! and arrange them in albums. You can also share albums with friends or with anyone who has a Yahoo! account.

Real Estate – Search for homes for sale by various criteria, or sell or rent your own property. Yahoo!'s Real Estate section also lets you research home values and neighborhoods, locate agents and movers, and get information on mortgages and insurance. You will also find tables of mortgage rates and a variety of loan calculators.

Search the Web – Search a database of more than 3 billion Web pages. Even if Yahoo! consisted of nothing but this search feature, serious searchers should still use it because of the size and quality of the database and the searching options provided. Links above the search box on Yahoo!'s home page also provide searches of Yahoo!'s large databases of Images, Local (Yellow Page listings), News, Products, and Web Directory listings. The Advanced Search link provides access to the more sophisticated options for refining and enhancing your searches. Chapter 2 discusses Yahoo! Search in detail.

Shopping – Shop at one of the world's largest and most easily searchable online shopping sites, with millions of products and more than 17,000 merchants. For details on Yahoo! shopping, see Chapter 7.

Sports – Read sports news and commentary, and participate in message boards, chat, groups, and fantasy sports. Within the Sports section are subsections for each major sport. Coverage is predominantly U.S., but you will find links to news and other information on non-U.S. sports and teams. You can customize the Sports page to include news and scores for your favorite teams.

Travel – Make airline, train, rental car, and cruise reservations, book vacation packages, and take advantage of a good collection of country and city travel guides. Chapter 9 contains more information about Yahoo! Travel.

TV – Find out what's on TV and when. You can personalize Yahoo!'s TV listings to spotlight your local providers and the channels you choose. You can browse the listings by day and time or search for specific content. Chapter 3 talks more about personalizing your Yahoo! TV listings.

Weather – Find detailed weather information worldwide. You can search by location and get current conditions, a five-day forecast, an extended forecast, maps, records, and averages for any large (or not so large) city. Yahoo! Weather also provides videos, maps, and images. You can get forecasts, alerts, and bulletins delivered via e-mail and to your mobile devices. Chapter 9 has more on Yahoo! Weather.

Web Site Directory – Browse the Web Site Directory. This is what gave Yahoo! its start. The directory contains around 2 million selected sites arranged in categories and subcategories; you can browse down through increasingly specific listings until you find the sites relevant to your needs. The original idea behind Yahoo!'s directory was that, since the sites are selected by human beings, you would generally end up with higher-quality sites than you would by using a search engine. However, as search engine results have improved in relevance and specificity over the last few years, human-constructed directories have lost considerable popularity. They are still useful, however, particularly when all you want is a few selected items on a fairly general topic. Chapter 2 discusses the Web Site Directory in detail.

Yellow Pages – Use this and Yahoo!'s Local Search to find businesses by category and by location. See Chapter 3 for more on Yellow Pages and Local Search.

SIGNING UP FOR YAHOO!

In general, signing up once covers most Yahoo! services—Yahoo! Mail, My Yahoo!, GeoCities, Groups, Auctions, etc.—although, as you move from one service to another for the first time, you might be required to answer a few additional questions. The information you supply when you first sign up serves several purposes. It establishes an identity for you, including a name by which you will be known on Yahoo! and to people with whom you communicate through Yahoo!. It also tells Yahoo! who you are (assuming you've answered truthfully). It identifies your language and location for automatic personalization of some services such as weather and local search. Answering Yahoo!'s "security question" will enable you to retrieve your password should you forget it. Finally, you won't be surprised to hear that it provides some marketing information so that Yahoo! can deliver more focused ads. (There *will* be ads, so be happy that they are focused). The sign-up page also gives you a chance to activate a Yahoo! Mail account if you haven't already done so.

For some services, particularly those that involve use of sensitive personal information such as credit card numbers, you will also be required to establish a second-level password that Yahoo! calls a Security Key. To access more sensitive areas, such as Bill Pay, Yahoo! will ask for your Security Key. When you are logged on to Yahoo! but have been inactive for a specified period of time, you may be required to enter your password again for security reasons.

You will also be asked for your password when you attempt to access your Yahoo! account information and your profile. All of these extra steps are indeed "protections," intended to prevent someone else from accessing or changing your personal data.

ACCOUNTS AND PROFILES

The sign-up procedure establishes your Yahoo! ID, a Yahoo! Account, and a Yahoo! Profile (see Figure 1.2). You can change almost all of this information later, except for your ID, by clicking the Account link found near the top of most Yahoo! pages. On the Account page, you can change your data by clicking the Edit buttons next to Member Information and Address/Contact Information.

From the Account page and some other pages, you can use the Edit/Create Profile link to change your Profile information. This is

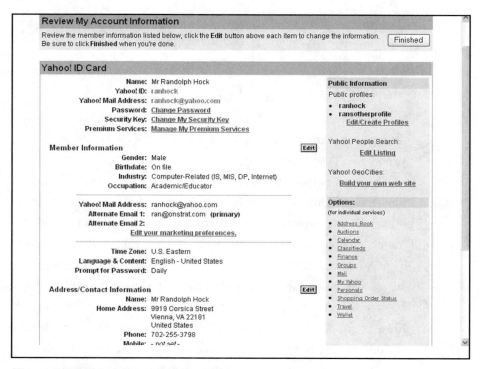

Figure 1.2 Yahoo! Account Information

the information about you that other Yahoo! users may see. You can actually create up to six additional profiles, with an alias for each that can be used instead of your regular Yahoo! ID. You might want to use an alias, for example, in Yahoo! Chat Rooms or Groups. Each profile can contain different information, depending on the context. For example, if you participate in a genealogy group, you might want other genealogy buffs to know something about you that would not be of interest to members of other groups in which you participate. Your profile might contain your real name, nickname, location, age, gender, marital status, occupation, e-mail address, hobbies, latest news, favorite quote, home page, and up to three other links. You can also choose to have your profile listed in the Yahoo! Member Directory (see next section). If you are very sensitive about your privacy, you can opt to remain unlisted, and your profile might contain only your Yahoo! ID.

Parents can also set up special Yahoo! accounts for children under the age of 13. To set up a Family Account, go to the Yahoo! Family Accounts page at family.yahoo.com. That page also provides a collection of resources to help kids and families use the Internet safely.

YAHOO! MEMBER DIRECTORY

You can click to the Member Directory from various locations throughout Yahoo!, or get to it directly by going to members. yahoo.com (see Figure 1.3).

The main purpose of this page is to allow you to search or browse the Member Directory. The Browse Interests links let you search for other Yahoo! members with particular interests. Find People on Yahoo! enables you to search by real name, Yahoo! ID, or interest. The Advanced Member Search link lets you do a more refined search using combinations of first name, last name, e-mail address, keywords, gender, age range, marital status, and location. You can limit your search to profiles that include pictures, or to people who are online at present. You can also create and edit your own profiles by clicking on View My Profiles. Additionally, you can tap into

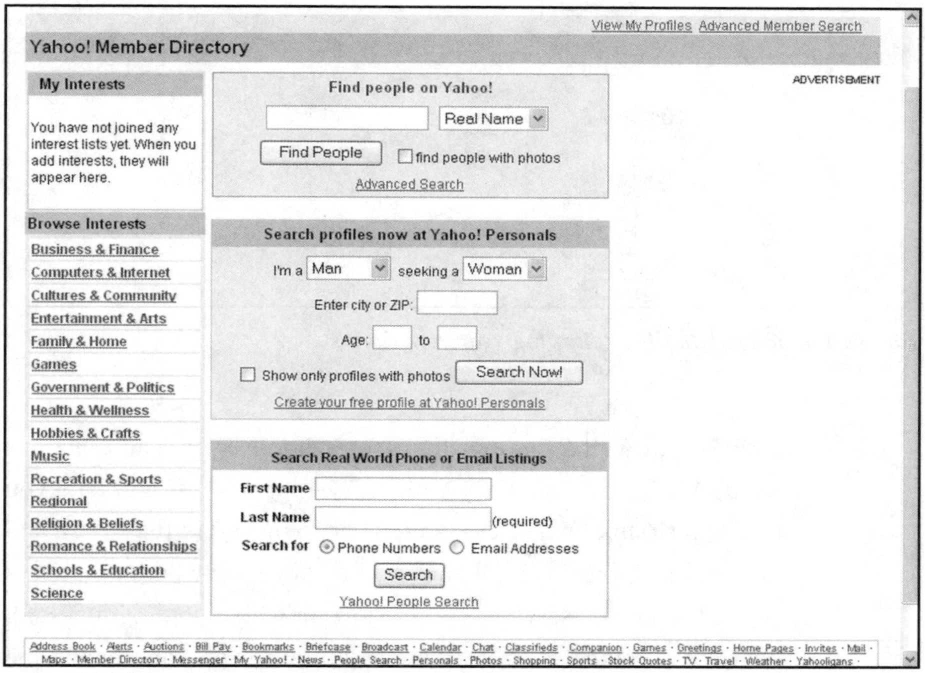

Figure 1.3 Yahoo! Member Directory

Yahoo!'s People Search service through the portion of the page labeled Search Real World Phone or E-mail Listings.

YAHOO! TOOLBAR

The Yahoo! Toolbar is a utility you can download and install on your browser (see Figure 1.4). You will find links for doing so throughout Yahoo!, or you can go directly to toolbar.yahoo.com. The Toolbar works with Windows 95, 98, ME, 2000, or XP and Internet Explorer 6.0 or later. It requires about 3 MB of space on your computer and, with a high-speed connection, should take about four minutes to download and install. It is well worth it.

The Yahoo! Toolbar gives you one- or two-click access to almost all of Yahoo!'s major areas and features, regardless of where you are on the Web. For example, you can always have the Yahoo! search box in view. Once you have installed the Toolbar, you will see the

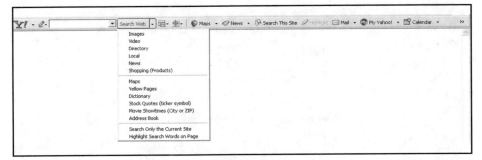

Figure 1.4 Yahoo! Toolbar (showing search options)

search box as well as buttons for other Yahoo! services and sections such as Mail, News, and My Yahoo!. The big red 'Y' will take you to the main Yahoo! page. The pencil icon to the left of the search box lets you customize the Toolbar by adding or deleting buttons, choosing just the Yahoo! services and sections in which you're interested. You have a choice of more than 70 buttons. You can change the order of the buttons and the width of the search box, display icons only versus icons *and* text, turn the anti-spy feature on or off, and enable, disable, or clear the display of recent searches. You can also select either of two alternate Toolbars: the Search and the Finance. Opt for one of them and you get a selection of Toolbar buttons specifically chosen for the search function or for Yahoo! Finance options.

Click on the down-arrow to the right of a Toolbar button for quick access to the major functions or options for that feature. Some of the buttons provide features that go beyond what you can do in Yahoo!. The Highlight button, for example, will automatically highlight your most recent search terms on the page currently showing in your browser.

The Yahoo! Toolbar provides two other functions that go beyond your use of Yahoo! itself. Built into the Toolbar program are a pop-up blocker and anti-spy software. The former blocks annoying pop-up ads. The latter helps prevent spyware or adware from being downloaded to your computer. Adware and spyware are programs that, usually without your knowledge, can capture and send information from your computer to a third party, often for malicious or other unpleasant purposes.

If you really want to use Yahoo! to the ultimate degree, give the Toolbar a try. If you decide you don't want it to be visible at all times, you can go to View > Toolbars in your browser and unclick Yahoo! Toolbar.

YAHOO! HELP

Yahoo! has done a good job with its Help pages. The Help link is context-sensitive and, in most cases, takes you directly to information that is precisely related to the page you are on. The Help Central link that you'll find on many Yahoo! pages is a gateway to more detailed help. The information on help screens is well-written and usually achieves a nice balance between brevity and completeness. Take advantage of Yahoo!'s Help pages and click on Help frequently to learn more about the site and what it has to offer. Be aware, though, that you will occasionally run into Help pages that are not up-to-date and that sometimes even refer to content or features that are no longer available.

PREMIUM SERVICES

On your travels through Yahoo!, you occasionally will bump into links and references to Premium services. These are services to which you must subscribe, or that you pay for as you use them. The Internet has conditioned some of us to the idea that everything online should be free, but don't be too quick to reject the idea of paying for some added-value services. What you get may well be worth the cost. Click the Premium Services link on the home page for an idea of what's available. Examples of Yahoo! Premium services are personal ads and classifieds, Wall Street research, Web site hosting, e-commerce storefronts, and college sports broadcasts. You'll often find special deals or free-trial offers. Even if you don't plan to buy, check out the Premium services that interest you; find out what they offer and how much they would cost. Though I emphasize the "free" aspects of Yahoo! in this book, some Premium services are extremely cost-effective and may provide services and content you can't readily get elsewhere.

SOME GENERAL POINTS

This chapter provides an overview of Yahoo! content and some concepts and features that apply throughout Yahoo!. The rest of the book discusses in detail specific Yahoo! sections, content, features, and options. If you have not already done so, I encourage you to read the Preface in order to better understand what to expect of this book and how to use it to your advantage.

Do keep in mind that with Yahoo!, the whole is indeed greater than the sum of its parts. Yahoo! is not just a collection of independent offerings. Features often become more valuable because they are leveraged with other Yahoo! resources. For example, Yahoo! News is greatly enhanced by the option of receiving news alerts via e-mail or Yahoo! Messenger.

Obviously, I am greatly impressed with Yahoo! or I would not have written this book. But Yahoo! is not perfect. Occasionally things don't work, or at least not as they should. Perhaps the content of the Calendar or Note Pad doesn't appear on your screen as it should. Maybe you encounter an error in the documentation or help file. It could be that an item or option you're looking for within Yahoo! no longer exists, or has changed its name or location. Almost certainly you'll run into problems like these now and then. Overall, though, especially considering Yahoo!'s extensive range of features and content, such glitches are rare. By and large, Yahoo! will do what you expect when you expect it.

As was mentioned and will be mentioned again, to really "get the max" from Yahoo!, take every opportunity to *explore*—and whenever you can, *click everywhere*.

CHAPTER 2

Searching and Browsing the Web with Yahoo!

In the beginning, circa 1994, Yahoo!'s main purpose was locating reliable, high-quality Web sites devoted to particular topics. A user could either browse through the Yahoo! directory or search it by means of a search box. Yahoo! has changed a lot since the early days. The directory, for a long time the centerpiece of the site, has become less and less prominent on Yahoo!'s home page. In 1996 Yahoo! began to incorporate access to a much larger database of Web sites, gathered by crawling the Web and not categorized like the original directory. For this broader searching function, Yahoo! has used, at various times, the databases of Inktomi, AltaVista, and Google. In 2004 it began using a database of its own for the search function, while still maintaining the directory database.

Though they appear pretty well integrated from the user's perspective, the two functions—*searching* a large Web database and *browsing* a much smaller collection of selected sites—are still separate and distinct within Yahoo! This chapter looks at how you can get the best from both.

YAHOO!, THE SEARCH ENGINE

You can get to Yahoo!'s search function via several different routes: the search box on Yahoo!'s main page, the search box on the Yahoo! Toolbar, the search module on My Yahoo!, or the Yahoo!

Search home page at search.yahoo.com. You may find additional routes on your own, as you explore Yahoo!. Whichever route you choose, Yahoo! will search the terms you enter against its database of more than 4 billion Web pages. As with other large search engine databases, most of these have been identified by a "crawler," a program that goes out to currently known Web pages, checking for new links. Yahoo!'s database also includes pages from its Content Acquisition Program. These pages have been supplied by various Yahoo! partners, such as National Public Radio (NPR), the New York Public Library, and the Online Computer Library Center (OCLC). These entities deliver records from their own databases that, in most cases, would not be discovered by crawler programs. Information like this is part of what is often referred to as the "invisible Web," and the fact that you can find it using Yahoo! adds a lot of value to the service.

In addition, Yahoo!'s search facility includes specialized databases for images, businesses, phone numbers, news, products, and maps. You can also choose to search just the Yahoo! Directory, as opposed to the broader Web database, for selected Web sites.

Figure 2.1 Yahoo! Search Home Page

One way to start understanding Yahoo!'s searching capabilities is to take a close look at the main search home page at search.yahoo.com (see Figure 2.1). On the main portion of this page you'll see the following:

- **The search box** – Allows you to enter one or more terms, and make your search more specific by using various connectors and prefixes.
- **The Advanced Search link** – Allows you to apply a number of additional search qualifications such as language, country, date, and domain.
- **The Language Tools link** – Allows you to search by language, country, or within a particular "local" Yahoo!, such as Yahoo! Brazil. This page also links to all the local Yahoo!s and a translation feature.
- **Services and Tools** – Provides links for searching the alternate Yahoo! databases such as Images and News, plus access to Search Shortcuts, the Toolbar, Search IMVironment (for chatting and searching with others), and other Yahoo! features. This page also has links for submitting your site to Yahoo! and adding a Yahoo! search box to your own site.

Above the search box are links for searching Images, Directory, Local, News, and Products. Additional search options are Maps, People Search, and Travel. Click on the Edit link to customize your selection.

Search Features for Yahoo!'s Search Home Page

You can refine your search on the Advanced Search page or by entering connectors and prefixes directly in the search box on Search home, Companion, My Yahoo!, or wherever you encounter it. Yahoo! gives you many options for making your search more precise.

Phrases

To search for a phrase (a specific string of two or more words in a specific order), enclose it in quotation marks. Phrase searching often produces much more relevant results. For example:

- "human resources"
- "tony blair"
- "king of hearts"

Boolean Logic

Boolean logic is a way to identify documents that have a particular combination of characteristics. For example, it allows you to specify that you only want those pages that contain the word "sailing" and also contain either the word "Chesapeake" or the word "Maryland." This approach usually uses AND, OR, and NOT, or equivalent symbols such as plus and minus signs, to define the relationship between words. AND means that both (or all) words must appear. OR means that either (or any) word must appear. NOT eliminates documents that contain a particular word, even if other desired words are present.

Here's how to use Boolean logic in Yahoo!:

AND – In Yahoo!, *all* words you enter are automatically ANDed together, unless you specify otherwise. If you enter:

sailing Chesapeake Maryland

you will get only those pages that contain all three words.

OR – If *either* of two or more words can occur in the documents you want, just type OR between them. OR is a good way to account for synonyms or related words. If your search combines an AND relationship with an OR relationship, you must add parentheses around your alternate (OR) words. For instance, you would enter:

sailing (chesapeake OR maryland)

Let's make this a little more complex. Suppose you want to find pages that deal with either "sailing" or "cruising" as well as referring to either "chesapeake" or "maryland" as the location. You would enter:

(sailing OR cruising) (chesapeake OR maryland)

NOT – To eliminate pages that contain a particular word, place a minus sign immediately in front of the undesired word. For example, to get information on Java, the programming language, and exclude those that refer to coffee, enter:

java –coffee

Searching Fields (Parts of Pages)

Field searching on the Web means searching for items that contain your word or words in a particular part of the page, such as the title, site name, or URL. Searching by field is one of the best ways to quickly get precise results. For example, if you are searching for information on meningitis, you can retrieve highly relevant items by asking for only those Web pages that have that word in their title.

To limit your retrieval by fields in Yahoo!, enter your word preceded by the appropriate prefix, such as intitle, site, or inurl. The following prefixes can be used in Yahoo!'s home page search box.

Title

To limit to title, use the intitle: prefix.

intitle:meningitis

If you want two or more words to appear in the title, use the allintitle: prefix.

allintitle:meningitis symptoms

To search for a phrase in the title, use the intitle: prefix and place your phrase in quotation marks:

intitle: "meningitis symptoms"

Site

To limit your retrieval to a particular Web site, use the site: prefix. This is similar to doing a "site search" when you're actually at that site, but it works even when the site doesn't offer a site search option. There is no guarantee that Yahoo! has indeed indexed every page on any given site, but this approach sometimes turns up more pages than the site's own "site search" feature.

To find all the pages that Yahoo! has indexed from the Embassy of Latvia in Washington, D.C., enter:

site:www.latvia-usa.org

More realistically, you would use a site search in conjunction with one or more additional search terms. To find references to travel on the Latvian Embassy site, enter:

travel site:www.latvia-usa.org

The site: prefix finds all pages from a particular domain, such as chrysler.com, and its subdomains, such as chile.chrysler.com.

You can also use the site: prefix to limit search results to a top-level domain (.edu, .com, .gov, .net, .org, .mil, .uk, .to, .biz, .info and so on). To find information from educational institutions on the ethics of human cloning, you can enter:

human cloning ethics site:edu

URL

Searching by URL (Uniform Resource Locator, or Web address) is very similar to site searching, except that you use the inurl: prefix to specify a *portion* of a URL. To get all pages with "avian" as part of the URL, enter:

inurl:avian

This would retrieve pages from www.avian-products.com, www.avian-vet.com, http://animalscience.ucdavis.edu/avian/ducks.pdf, www.avian.net, and www.cdc.gov/flu/avian/, among others.

You can also use the allinurl: prefix for multiple words in the URL. For example, to get documents from the Russian embassy, enter:

allinurl:embassy ru

Link

Link searching enables you to identify pages that link *to* a particular page. This can be very powerful for competitive intelligence research, since it enables you to discover what other entities have a particular interest in a given product, service, company, organization, or issue. Link searching is also useful for finding sites that relate in some way to a page you've already found, since a link to a page can indicate similar interests and topics. Searching for links has numerous other applications as well.

To do a link search in Yahoo!, use the link: prefix. Be aware that you must include the "http://" part of the Web address or URL. You may also want to try variations on the URL. To see what pages link to the Federation of American Scientists Web site, enter one of the following:

link:http://fas.org OR link:http://www.fas.org

File Type

Yahoo! indexes not only ordinary Web pages written in HTML, but documents in several other file formats as well, including Adobe PDF (.pdf), Microsoft Excel (.xls), Word (.doc), PowerPoint (.ppt), XML/RSS (.xml, .rdf, .rss), and plain text (.txt). Limiting by file type is helpful in a variety of situations. If you want to print out a tutorial on a certain software package, you might prefer the more attractive Adobe PDF format. If you are called upon to do a quick presentation on a topic, you might find PowerPoint presentations available for public use. If you are looking for statistical data on a particular commodity, try limiting your search to Excel files.

Though Yahoo! at one point had (and may have again) a "file-type:" prefix that could be used similarly to the other prefixes mentioned, it removed that capability. To search for a particular type of file, instead make use of the "File Format" option on Yahoo!'s Advanced Search page.

Host Name

Yahoo! also supports the hostname: prefix, which is similar to the site: prefix, but is intended to retrieve only pages from a specific subdomain, such as chile.chrysler.com. You'll get better results if you use the site: prefix.

No matter which of the search methods discussed in this section you use, Yahoo! Search is not case-sensitive, so whether you enter Smith or smith does not matter.

Advanced Search Page

The Advanced link on Yahoo!'s home page, on the main Yahoo! Search page, and elsewhere, enables you to use Boolean and field searching without having to remember the syntax (see Figure 2.2).

The Advanced Search page handles Boolean searching by inviting you to enter your search terms in the "all of these words," "any of these words," or "none of these words" boxes, as appropriate, in the "Show results with" section of the page. Going back to our "sailing on the Chesapeake" example, you can type sailing in the "all of these words" box, and both maryland and chesapeake in the "any of these words" box. This will produce the same result as entering sailing (chesapeake OR maryland) in Yahoo!'s basic search box. On the Advanced Search page, you can type alternate terms for more than one of the concepts in the "any of the words" box:

(sailing OR cruising) (chesapeake OR maryland)

To confine your search term to the title or URL, use the pull-down menu on the right of the "Show results with" section and choose either "in the title of the page" or "in the URL of the page."

The Updated option on the Advanced Search page theoretically enables you to limit retrieval to Web pages published "anytime," "within the past 3 months," "within the past 6 months," or "within the past year." I say "theoretically" because date searching does not really work for Web pages the way it does with printed books and periodicals. Web pages typically do not include a reliable publication date, let alone in a form that search engines can read. Modifying a page, however slightly, can change its apparent publication date.

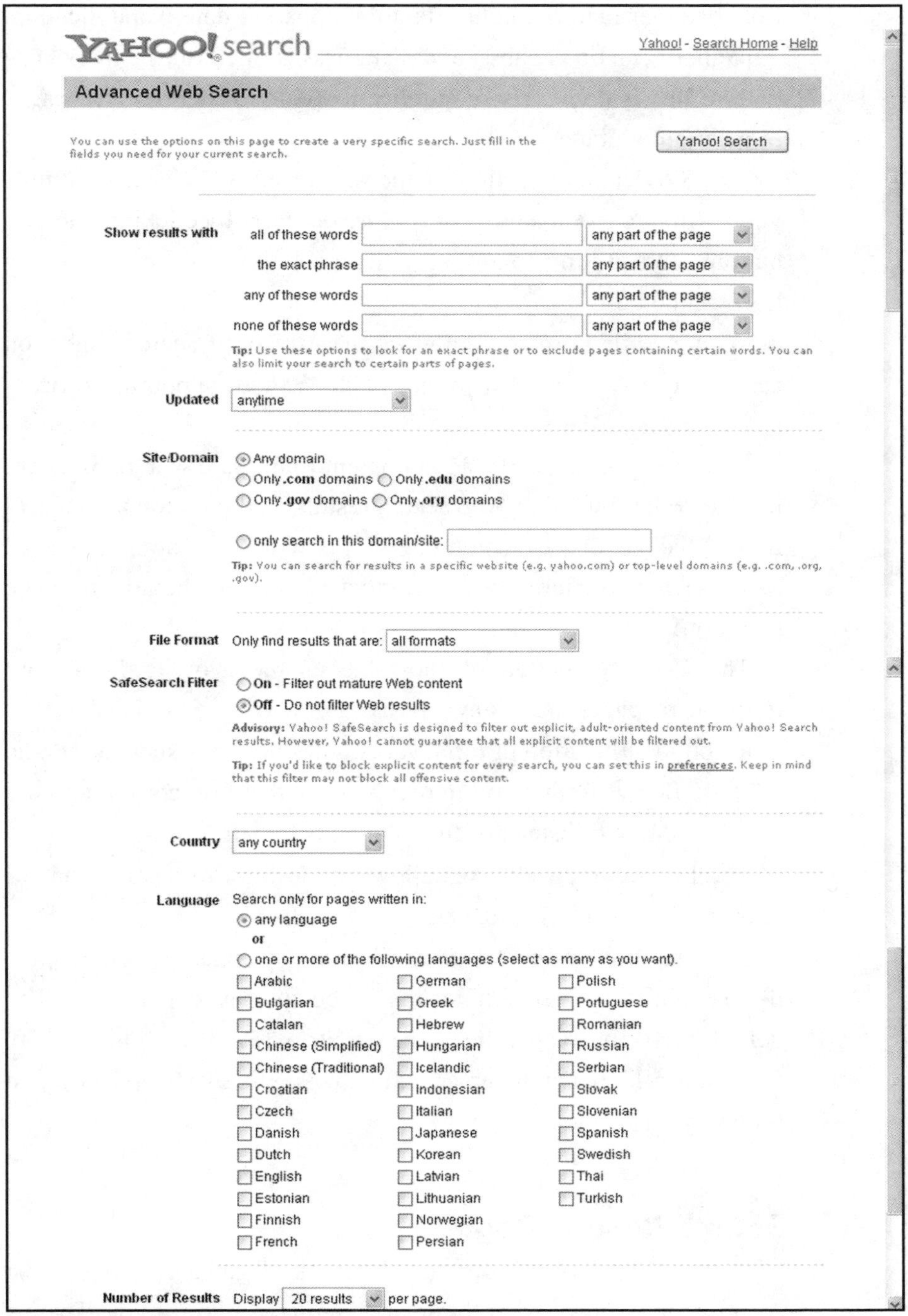

Figure 2.2 Yahoo! Advanced Search Page

Lots of other factors might affect the apparent date of publication. All Yahoo! can do is guess, and that guess is often off the mark. The bottom line is don't rely on publication date to retrieve Web pages of a certain vintage.

The Site/Domain section of the Advanced Search page permits you to limit to .com, .edu, .gov, or .org domains by clicking on radio buttons, and to limit to any specific site or domain by entering its URL in the box.

With the File Format window on the Advanced Search page, you can restrict your retrieval to any of the Yahoo! supported formats talked about earlier.

You can apply Yahoo!'s adult content filter, SafeSearch, by clicking the "Filter out adult Web search results" radio button in that section of the Advanced Search page. This will not guarantee that all adult-oriented material will be blocked, but it should eliminate much of it.

The Country section of the page enables you to limit your retrieval to pages from any of two-dozen countries. This feature relies on identification of top level country domains such as .fr, .de, and .uk. Be aware that you may miss sites that use .com or another top level domain instead of their country domain.

The Language checkboxes allow you to limit retrieval to one or more of thirty-eight languages.

The final box on the Advanced Search page enables you to specify the number of search results to be displayed per page. The default is 10, but you can increase that to 15, 20, 30, 40, or 100. Selecting a higher number generally makes it easier and faster to browse your results.

Search Results Page

A close look at a Yahoo! search results page can provide some surprises in terms of what the search engine can do for you. There's more to the results page than just delivering a list of links to information on your topic (see Figure 2.3).

Record Contents

The individual items on Yahoo!'s search results pages are listed in order of their relevance to the search terms you supplied. Relevance is based on a number of factors, including how prominently your terms appear on the page; occurrence in the title would rank more highly than a passing reference deep in the text of the document. Each item includes the title of the page (as a link) and a brief description. You'll also find a little "double page" icon that you can click to open that page in another window. Depending on the item, you might also find the following:

- **Category** – If the page is in the Yahoo! Directory, you will see a category, such as "Belarus > Country Guides," You can click on the category and go to that location in the Yahoo! Directory to see similar selected sites.
- **Cached** – Clicking on this link will take you to an archived copy of the page. If you click on the title of a page and the

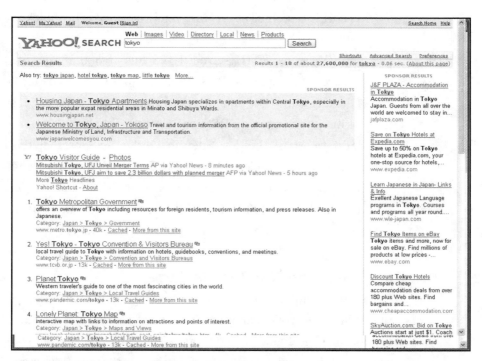

Figure 2.3 Yahoo! Search Results Page

page is no longer available, you can fall back on the cached copy. If the term you searched for doesn't appear on the page, that means the page might have changed since it was indexed by Yahoo!. In that case, click on "cached" and you might find your term on the older version of the page.

- **"More pages from this site"** – Yahoo! only shows the highest ranked page from any site. Click on this link to see other matching pages from the site.

- **"Translate this page"** – Pages in French, German, Italian, Portuguese, and Spanish offer a "Translate this page" link. Click to get a machine translation of the page. It might not be a perfect translation, but it could be adequate enough to give you a general idea of what the page is about. Keep in mind that the translation program can't translate words on a page that are part of an image and not the actual text.

- **View as HTML** – When you retrieve a page in PDF format (yes, that is redundant), Yahoo! serves up a "View as HTML" option. The HTML equivalent may be quicker, although it probably won't be as pretty.

- **RSS/View as XML** – You'll see this option if the site referred to supports RSS (Really Simple Syndication). Clicking will show you the XML code in which the page is written. (For more on RSS, see Chapter 5, Yahoo! News.)

- **Add to My Yahoo!** – Sites that offer RSS present this option as well. Select it to automatically add this source to the RSS headlines that appear on your My Yahoo! page. (For details, see Chapter 3, My Yahoo!: The Best General Portal on the Web.)

Other Items on the Results Page

It's easy to fall into the habit of looking only at the list of retrieved items on your search results page. After all, it *is* a results page. But the page contains a lot more. Depending on the topic you searched and the results, you might find any or all of the following:

- Links to Yahoo!'s searchable **Images**, **Directory**, **Local**, **News**, and **Products** databases – These are discussed in some detail in the next section.

- **Also try…** – This section lists other possible searches that use one or more of your search terms. "Also try" can provide useful suggestions to narrow or otherwise improve your search.

- **Did you mean…** – If you misspelled a word, or might have, Yahoo! graciously asks "Did you mean…?" and offers you a likely alternative. If it was indeed a mistake, just click on Yahoo!'s alternate suggestion to correct the problem.

- **News** – At the same time that Yahoo! searches the Web for you, it also checks its news database. If it finds matches for your search terms, you may see up to three headlines, plus links to additional stories.

- **Inside Yahoo!** – This section provides links to other portions of Yahoo! that may be relevant to your search. For example, when you search for a city or country, you might see links to a Visitor Guide, the World Factbook, photos, a Local City Guide, plus Yellow Pages, maps, and weather. A search on an actor might lead to that actor's page in Yahoo!'s Movies section, to photos, and to DVDs and videos. A search on a disease might reference a relevant page in Yahoo!'s Health section. Other topics will lead you to other sections within Yahoo! that may be of interest.

- **Sponsor Results** – These are ads linking to businesses and other entities that have paid to appear on Yahoo! results pages in response to certain keyword searches. Sponsor sites appear on a tinted background or off to the side of the page, or both, so you can easily distinguish them from your actual unpaid results.

Preferences

The Preferences link that appears on many Yahoo! pages allows you to set a number of search-related features. Preferences remain fixed from search to search until you go back and change them. Some preferences you can set are:

- **New Window** – Every link you click on will open in a new window. Useful when you want to compare pages you've retrieved, or keep track of where you've been on your results list.
- **Number of Results** – Allows you to display 10, 15, 20, 30, 40, or 100 results per page.
- **SafeSearch Filter** – You can choose to filter adult content from (a) Web, video, and image search results, (b) video and image search results, or (c) none of those results.
- **Language** – This is the same list of languages that you see on the Advanced Search page; here the setting is retained for all your searching, until you change it again.

Alternate Searchable Databases

The links you see near the search box on various Yahoo! pages indicate that you can also search Images, Directory, Local, News, Products, and perhaps video databases. On the Search home page, the Edit link lets you add up to three additional links: Maps, People Search, and Travel.

Image Search

You can do an image search by clicking on the Images link and then entering your search terms. Alternatively, click on Images after you've done a Web or other search. Yahoo! will then search your terms in the Images database. The database includes more than a billion images from sources included in Yahoo!'s Web database, as well as images from Yahoo! News and Yahoo! Movies.

You can enter one or more terms in an image search, and use quotation marks for phrases. You cannot use the minus sign to exclude a term or use the Boolean OR. Search engine crawlers typically index images under very few terms, which means that you shouldn't use more than one or two words to search for them; being overly specific will probably produce zero results.

Image search results pages tell you how many images were found and display thumbnail images for the first twenty (see Figure 2.4). Under each thumbnail is the file name of the image, the file size, its dimensions in pixels, and its Web page URL. Click on a thumbnail to see a "frames" page with a perhaps slightly larger version of the image, accompanied by the information you saw on the results page. If this image is scaled down, you'll get a link to the full-size version. The bottom frame consists of the Web page on which the image was found. You can get rid of the top frame by clicking the "Close Yahoo! frame" link.

Look for the Advanced Images Search link on your image search pages. This enables you to enhance your search in several ways. You can apply simple Boolean logic via the "all of these words," "any of these words," or "none of these words" boxes. You can also specify

Figure 2.4 Image Search Results

the size of the image you want (any size, wallpaper, large, medium, small), color (any color, color only, black and white only), site/domain (.com, .edu, .gov, .org, or a specific domain), and SafeSearch filter (on or off). The image results page also offers a SafeSearch link.

Directory

The Directory link allows you to search the Yahoo! Directory (the directory is discussed in detail at the end of this chapter). Briefly, this link allows you to search for "selected" Web sites, a far smaller database than you tap into with Yahoo! Search (see the section, Yahoo!, the Search Engine, earlier in this chapter). Sites in the Yahoo! Directory have been selected by humans, not by a Web crawler, and inclusion may be affected by whether the owner of a site has paid a fee to Yahoo!.

Yellow Pages and Local Search

The Yellow Pages search option has been sidelined a bit by the easier and better "Local Search." Local Search was one of several shortcuts available from the main search page, but, in 2004, Yahoo! introduced a more sophisticated version at local.yahoo.com. You can also get to it via links elsewhere in Yahoo!. In the shortcut approach, you enter a name or type of business (Saks, Blockbuster, plumber, pizza, interpreter, or whatever you're looking for) in the main Yahoo! search box, along with a U.S. city name plus two-letter postal code for a state. Yahoo! will process your entry as a regular Web search query and return a results list. In addition, if Yahoo! found matching businesses in its Yellow Pages database, it will display up to three listings at the top of the search results. Each listing includes the business name, phone number, address, distance from the location you specified, and a link to a map. You will also find links to view all "Local Results" and to view your results on a map.

The maps Yahoo! provides for Local Search are tremendously useful, with icons showing the location of each establishment. Click on any icon to get further details and to get a link for driving directions. The map pages also provide lists of links corresponding to the icons and the capability of zooming in or out on the map.

If you start your search from the Local Search page at local.yahoo.com, you'll see a "Search for:" box, in which you enter the type of business, and a "Location:" box, in which you enter address, city and state, or ZIP. If you are signed in to Yahoo!, the Location: box automatically shows the location you specified in your Yahoo! profile. Results pages don't show Web results, just a list of matching businesses. Each entry includes the business name, address, phone number, a link to the company's Web site if it has one, a rating based on input by Yahoo! users, a link to a map, and the distance from the address you specified. Click on any business name and you get more detailed information, including cross streets and a map that you can enlarge. You can further tailor the map to show nearby ATMs, hotels, parking, public transportation, and hospitals. There's also a link to driving directions.

You can refine your local search by distance and by business category. You can also sort results alphabetically, or by distance, rating, and other criteria depending on the type of establishment. A "restaurant" search will allow you to refine by "atmosphere," for instance, but a "hardware store" search will not.

Yahoo! stores your recent search locations in a pull-down list accessible by using the button to the right of the Location box. You can clear the locations you've searched on, or save any of them permanently, which comes in handy if you travel regularly to certain locations.

Clicking the Yellow Pages link, either before or after entering terms in the search box, gives you access to additional business category breakdowns and the opportunity to extend your search beyond your original location (at least it did when this book went to press). Expect to see further changes in Local Search, the Yellow Pages, and Maps since Yahoo! and its competitors are busily working on innovations in this area. For more detail on Maps, see Chapter 9, Other Seriously Useful Yahoo! Stuff.

News

If you enter terms in the search box and click the News link, Yahoo! will run your search in its News database, which covers more than 7,000 news sources in 35 languages. For a full discussion of news searching, see Chapter 5, Yahoo! News.

Products

Entering a product name in the search box and clicking the Products link will run your search in the Yahoo! Shopping database. See Chapter 7, Buying and Selling through Yahoo!, for details.

Video

You will find the link to Yahoo!'s new Video search in a number of places or you can go directly to video.yahoo.com. Yahoo!'s Video Search is structured very similarly to its Image Search. Enter one or more search terms, click the Search Video button, and results pages will show thumbnail frames, sizes, and URL's for up to 20 videos (with links at the bottom of the page for more). As with images, more than two terms are likely to give zero results. From the results pages, when you click on one of the thumbnails, you will be given a page with information about the video at the top of the screen and a frame with the original source page at the bottom.

With the Advanced Video Search page, you can limit your search by format (AVI, MPEG, Quicktime, Windows Media, or Real), size (small, medium, large), duration (less than or more than one minute), and domain (any, .com, .edu, .gov., .org, or another specific domain or site). A SafeSearch Filter option is also provided. A Preferences link provides the same preference settings as in a Web search (open results in a new window, number of results, filtering level, and language).

The "Edit" Option

Adjacent to the Web and alternate database links just described, you'll see an "Edit" link. This allows you to add or remove database links on Yahoo!'s Search page. In addition to the default choices

(Web, Images, Directory, Local, News, Products), you can add Maps, People Search, and Travel. You can also delete links from your Search page that you don't use very often.

Maps

Click on the Maps link and you get a search page with a box for "Address" and a box for "City, State or Zip." Enter a complete address, or just city and state or ZIP code, click the Search button, and Yahoo! displays a map of the location you entered. Yahoo! map currently works for U.S. and Canadian locations only. For more details on Yahoo! Maps, see Chapter 9.

People Search

Clicking on People Search takes you to a form for locating a telephone number within the U.S. or an e-mail address. Phone number searches require at least a last name. E-mail address searches require either a first or a last name. Results come from Yahoo!'s telephone and e-mail directories (people.yahoo.com). For more details on Yahoo! People Search, see Chapter 9.

Travel

The Travel link takes you to a quick search for airline flights, with a form for entering your departure and destination cities, departure and return dates, number of travelers, and number of connections you are willing to tolerate. Results are from Yahoo! Travel (travel.yahoo.com), with flight information, bookings, etc., provided by Yahoo!'s FareChase service. See Chapter 9 for further discussion of Yahoo! Travel.

Shortcuts

Beyond the kinds of searches discussed earlier in this chapter, you can perform numerous cool tricks and shortcuts right in Yahoo!'s main search box. Click the Shortcuts or View All Shortcuts link, wherever you might see it, to keep up on the latest. Yahoo! is constantly adding new shortcuts, but try the following shortcuts for starters.

Calculator

For a quick arithmetic calculation, instead of pulling up a calculator, just enter your problem in Yahoo!'s search box. If you need to multiply 456 by 56.98, type 456*56.98, hit the search button, and your answer will appear at the top of the page. To add, subtract, multiply, and divide, use +, -, *, and /, respectively. For exponents use ^ (for example, 10^6). You can do more complex calculations using parentheses, as in the example, 15*(14+43).

Conversions

As long as the U.S. continues to avoid the metric system and sticks so unilaterally to the medieval, arcane, isolationist, and reactionary Imperial system of measure (not that I have a strong opinion on this matter), we will occasionally need to convert between the two systems. If you happen to love the numeric relationships between inches, feet, yards, miles, and rods, or between bushels, pecks, and quarts, forget I said anything. To easily find equivalents between metric and Imperial measures, type the word "convert" in Yahoo!'s main search box, followed by the conversion you want to do. For example, type "convert 8.2 miles to kilometers," "convert 2 mi to in," "convert 3°C to Fahrenheit." The conversion shortcut works for most common units of length, weight, temperature, area, and volume. You can generally use the full term or an abbreviation, and either singular or plural units (for example, inch or inches).

Other Shortcuts

Most of Yahoo!'s other search shortcuts are fairly intuitive, given their name and an example. Some involve simply entering a number or term in the search box. Some require a prefix or suffix such as "time in" or "weather." For regional queries such as movie showtimes, Yahoo! might assume the location shown in your Yahoo! profile. Getting the answer sometimes requires one more click to get to the appropriate database.

The Format column in Table 2.1 shows the form in which to enter your query. The variable portion—the specific data you're searching for—is in italics. The Examples column gives an illustration of what an actual query might look like.

Most of the shortcuts work very well, but some, such as UPC codes, will tend to frequently strike out.

Searching with a Partner

Suppose you're planning a vacation with a friend in another city, or working from home on a research project and need to confer with a colleague. You can take advantage of Yahoo! Messenger's Search IMVironment to collaborate on a search. Both of you can see the results at the same time and each can modify the search. For details on searching with a partner, see Chapter 6, Yahoo!: The Great Communicator.

Yahoo! Toolbar

If you've installed the Yahoo! Toolbar, virtually everything on the Search home page is available to you without having to navigate there with your browser. The one major exception, strangely, is Advanced Search, but you can add it yourself, using one of the Toolbar's "Your Own Button" choices.

The Toolbar makes a number of search-related tasks easier. Try "Search Only the Current Site," an option in the pull-down menu next to the "Search Web" button. The Toolbar also allows you to double-click on any word that's not a link on a Web page, then right-click and choose "Search Web for [that term]." Yahoo! then executes the search. Clicking the Toolbar's Highlight button will highlight your most recent search terms on the current page.

Table 2.1 Shortcuts

Type of Information	Format	Example
Aircraft Registration	*FAA Reg. number*	n4021e
Airport Information	*city/airport code* airport	lax airport
Area Codes (area covered by)	*area code*	408
Book Price Finder	*ISBN*	0910965684
Dictionary Definitions	define *word*	define obstreperous
Encyclopedia Lookup	topic *name*	topic entropy
Exchange Rate	convert *currency1* to *currency2*	convert 200 dollars to euros
Flight Tracker	*airline flight #*	united 127
Gas Prices (by ZIP code)	gas *ZIP*	gas 10017
Hotel Finder	*city* hotels	baltimore hotels
Maps	*address city state*	9919 corsica street vienna va
Movie Showtimes	showtimes *ZIP code*	showtimes 67201
News	news t*opic*	news medicare
Package Tracker (FedEx, UPS, USPS)	*Service tracking number*	FedEx 46388764903
Sports Scores	*team* scores	cubs scores
Stock Quotes	quote *ticker symbol*	quote intc
Synonym Finder	synonym *word*	synonym hairy
Time Zones	time in *city*	time in Vienna
Traffic Reports	*city* traffic	seattle traffic
UPC Code	*UPC code*	*048001265165*
U.S. Patents	*Patent Number*	patent 1034383253
Vehicle History	*Vehicle Identification Number*	SCCFE33C9VHF64857
Weather	*city* weather	dallas weather
Yellow Pages	*business city state*	dentist chestertown md
ZIP Codes	ZIP code *city*	zip code buffalo

Get in the habit of using Yahoo!'s Toolbar and searching will be even easier. For details on the toolbar, see Chapter 1, Yahoo!'s Home Page: An Overview of Yahoo!.

BROWSING THE WEB: THE YAHOO! DIRECTORY

There is something almost sad and a bit ironic now about discussing the Yahoo! Web Site Directory. At one point the directory *was* Yahoo!. For much of Yahoo!'s life, the directory was its most obvious and most popular feature, its *raison d'etre*. Since 2001 the directory has been, as they say in the newspaper world, "below the fold," not visible unless you scroll down Yahoo!'s main page. Nostalgia aside, the directory does still serve a purpose, although that purpose has been largely eclipsed by Yahoo!'s search and portal functions.

The purpose that the directory did and still does serve is *browsing*—the ability to look through an organized collection of selected sites, in contrast to *searching* a much larger database of nonselective Web pages. As you drill down from broader to more restrictive categories in the directory hierarchy, you narrow the focus of your search. This approach can be particularly useful when you're not sure, initially, how to make your search more precise, or when you're not familiar with the overall subject area. The directory approach is also useful when all you want is a few good sites.

The advantage of a well-constructed Web directory like Yahoo!'s is that everything in it has been selected by a (presumably) intelligent human and arranged in categories that guide you to more and more precise listings, even if you don't know quite what you're looking for to begin with. Directories are smaller than search engine databases, since their purpose is ostensibly to identify only the better resources on any given topic, and since the selection process takes time and is more expensive than using a software crawler. The Yahoo! directory contains about 2 million sites, versus the 3 billion or so pages in the Yahoo! Web search database. If you're really paying attention here, you may have picked up on another distinction: Directories, Yahoo!'s among them, usually index *sites*— often just the home page of a site—while search engines index *pages*, often multiple pages in a single site.

Categories

To use Yahoo!'s directory, you can either search it via the Directory link associated with the Yahoo! Search box, or you can go to dir.yahoo.com (see Figure 2.5). The structure of the Yahoo! Directory is based on 14 main categories. Click on any category to see the next level of subcategories. Each of the main categories typically has three to six sublevels, for example: Science > Mathematics > Geometry > Computational Geometry > Trigonometry. At the second or third sublevel, you typically begin to see not just the next set of subcategories,

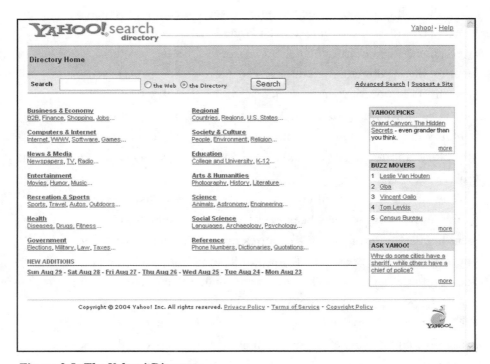

Figure 2.5 The Yahoo! Directory

but some actual site listings. Some of these may be "sponsored" (i.e., advertisements), others not.

Subcategory Pages

On a typical subcategory page (see Figure 2.6), you will see the following:

- A search box that allows you to search the Web or just within the current directory category. The "just this category" choice can provide a useful refinement. If you're looking for information on graphics from a graphics arts perspective rather than from the computer and Web end of things, you might start by browsing Arts and Humanities > Design Arts > Graphic Design. At that point, since you still have more than a thousand Yahoo! selected sites to deal with, use the search box to search for your specific needs

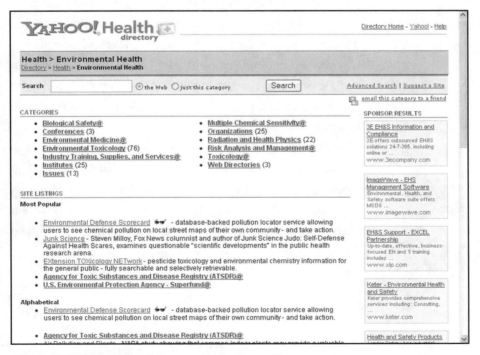

Figure 2.6 Yahoo! Web Directory Subcategory Page

within the current Graphic Design category. That way, you avoid bumping into many "techie" sites that may be irrelevant for your purposes. Starting from the Computers and Internet category instead, and branching into Graphics from there, would produce entirely different, much more technology-focused results.

- Near the top of each page in the directory hierarchy, Yahoo! reminds you where you are (for instance: Directory > Health > Environmental Health). You can click on the preceding levels to go back up one or more steps and broaden your search.

- The Categories section of each subcategory page shows what additional subcategories are available and how many listings appear in each. An @ sign next to a category indicates that it is a cross-reference for a category whose primary location is elsewhere in the hierarchy. In this example, shown in Figure 2.6, if you click on "Biological Safety," you will go to the page for Biology > Biological Safety.

- The Site Listings section of the page shows the sites that Yahoo! has classified at the current level of specificity. Clicking on one of these will take you to the actual site. In some cases, site listings include "Most Popular," followed by an alphabetical listing. Any "Sponsor Results" listed here are paid ads.

- "Inside Yahoo!" listings on some category pages take you to potentially relevant Yahoo! resources such as News and other Yahoo! areas such as Finance or Health. Depending on the topic, some category listings are divided in different ways, for example, by Commercial Categories, Region, and Top Categories.

SEARCHING AND BROWSING

This chapter has demonstrated how useful Yahoo!'s Web search, specialized search types such as Images, and added features, such as shortcut searches, can be. It's also shown why and when you might find that browsing through Yahoo!'s Directory is your best approach. These two main functions, searching and browsing, will become even more useful as you learn more about their capabilities and the variety of ways in which you can use them to find what you need. The secret to getting the most out of Yahoo! and maximizing its benefits is to *explore*. Look around constantly to see what you haven't used before. And *click everywhere* to see where it leads.

CHAPTER 3

My Yahoo!: The Best General Portal on the Web

THE PORTAL CONCEPT

A working definition of a general Web portal might be "a Web page or site that provides, in one place, immediate and easy access to a variety of tools and Internet resources, and is usually personalizable in order to enhance the value, usability, and relevance of content to individual users." That's a mouthful. More briefly, a portal is a page where you can quickly get to a variety of useful information. For that reason, general portals are also designed to make good start pages, or home pages, the page you go to automatically when you open your Web browser. The "general" in "general Web portal" is necessary to distinguish the kind of portal we'll be discussing here from specialized portals that focus on a particular industry, field of study, profession, or purpose.

There has been a lot of competition over the years in the general portal arena. Excite, Lycos, Netscape, and others have all produced general portal pages, with personalized versions usually distinguished from the nonpersonalized versions by the addition of "My" in front of the name (My Excite, My Lycos, and so on). None has succeeded as well as Yahoo! in offering a wide range of easily accessible resources and a great degree of personalization. My Yahoo! manages to integrate a broad variety of services and consolidate them nicely on a single page. My Yahoo! provides one- or two-click access to Yahoo! Mail, Chatrooms, News, the Yahoo! Calendar, and other services.

47

The portal concept regularly goes in and out of favor with Web marketing "experts" (the same experts who brought us the dot.com bubble), especially those on the search engine side. AltaVista was a search engine, then a portal as well, then not, ad infinitum. Though many users have been slow to notice, Google, the most "pure" search engine, with nothing but a search box on the home page, has been expanding into a wide range of other offerings (directory, news, images, shopping, local, etc.), even appearing to imitate Yahoo! in several ways.

PERSONALIZING MY YAHOO!

As we discussed in Chapter 1, Yahoo!'s main page (yahoo.com) provides access to a very extensive collection of resources. Some, such as news headlines, are just a single click away. Yahoo!'s main page is a portal, but not a personalized one. My Yahoo! takes some of Yahoo!'s resources as a starting point and lets you add and remove features depending upon your personal interests. Figure 3.1 shows a basic My Yahoo! page without any modification.

Once you have a regular Yahoo! account, you can go to My Yahoo! and use your user name and password to sign in. From the main Yahoo! page, click the "My" button at the top of the page to get to My Yahoo!. To get there directly, type my.yahoo.com in your browser's address box. On the sign-in page, click "Remember my ID" if you want to bypass the sign-in procedure in the future. To make My Yahoo! the start page for your browser, just click the "Set as homepage" link you will find in various places on My Yahoo!.

My Yahoo! starts you off with a front page that you can customize to match your interests (see Figure 3.2). You can also add additional pages, each of which you can personalize by adding modules of your choice. The personalization buttons near the top of the My Yahoo! page allow you to change the color scheme, select the content you want to appear on your page, change the layout (primarily the order in which content areas appear on your page), and add or delete pages.

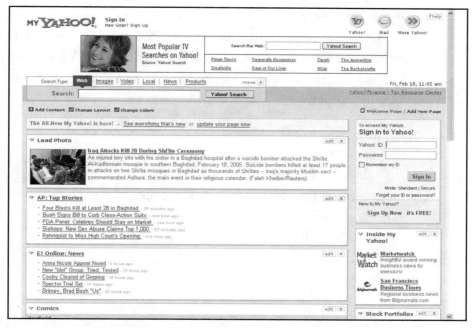

Figure 3.1 Basic My Yahoo! Page

In this chapter, we are discussing My Yahoo! as it appears in a main window on your computer screen. Once you have set it up though, the possibilities do not end there. My Yahoo! content can also be delivered to you through Yahoo! Messenger or on your mobile phone. Messenger is discussed in Chapter 6, Yahoo!, The Great Communicator, and for information on getting My Yahoo! on your mobile phone, go to mobile.yahoo.com.

Change Colors

This may be the least significant of My Yahoo!'s personalization options, but it's also the easiest to explain. Clicking on this button allows you to choose from scores of design themes, with various color combinations for headings, subheadings, and backgrounds, including picture backgrounds. The "Customize Theme" link lets you pick your own combination of colors.

Add Content

The Add Content button allows you to determine what kinds of information you want to appear on your page. Click on Add Content to browse through three general and thirteen subject-specific categories.

Yahoo! Services	Local
Editors' Picks	News & Media
Popular from the Web	Politics
Business & Finance	Recreation & Travel
Entertainment & Arts	Reference
Health & Wellness	Science
Internet & Technology	Shopping
Living & Lifestyles	Sports

Figure 3.2 Personalized My Yahoo! Page

Click on any of the categories and you will see up to 16 sub-categories, plus a list of the most popular modules for that category. Many modules are listed in more than one category. You can also locate modules of interest by making use of the Search box found on the Add Content pages. In addition to the 200,000 RSS news content sources, there are more than 100 other modules from which to choose and you can have up to 100 modules on your page. Later in this chapter I'll describe several dozen of the more popular modules in some detail. On the Add Content pages, you can click on the name of any module to get an example of the kind of service or information to expect. Also, a diagram on the left of each of those pages shows the current content and layout of your page. Hold your cursor over the diagram to identify the specific modules on your page. Click the Add or Remove buttons to add or remove modules from your page. As you explore the offerings of each category, be sure to look at the subcategories as well as the list of most popular modules.

When you've selected your modules, click the "Finish" button. Your page now reflects your content choices. You can delete a module either by going back to the Add Content page and removing it, or simply clicking the "X" button on the upper right of the module box.

Most modules on the My Yahoo! page also display an Edit button, which allows you to customize it further. For example, Weather offers a choice of cities, and Portfolios lets you select the stocks and indices you want to follow. For some modules, the Edit button allows you to add your own content. You can add files to Briefcase, enter your URL selections in Bookmarks, or put your own notes in Notepad.

Change Layout

The Change Layout page lets you choose either a two- or three-column layout. You can then move modules from one column to another or up or down on the page. This is very convenient, especially if you have chosen a large number of modules, since it allows you to put your favorite or most-used modules at the top of your page (see Figure 3.2).

Add New Page

The hundred-module limit will satisfy a lot of information needs. But if you want to add more, My Yahoo! can accommodate them with up to five additional pages. You might also want to create additional pages to focus on a particular area of interest. If you want, you can devote your My Yahoo! front page to items of general interest, and each additional page to a specialized area of interest.

To add a page, use the Add a New Page or the Select Page button on My Yahoo!. You can create your own page or use one of the eight "Packages": News, Fun, Business & Stock Quotes, Travel, Sports, Local Info, Entertainment, Connect & Organize. For any of these, you can select from all the content modules you find under Add Content. You can also give the page a name of your choice and, if you want, make any of the pages your default My Yahoo! page. When adding or deleting pages, you can also set the page refresh rate and rename any of your pages.

My Yahoo! Content

The essence of My Yahoo!'s value lies in the wide range of available content combined with the degree to which you can customize the content you want to see. In many cases, the names of the modules on the Add Content pages are self-explanatory. Movie Showtimes are movie showtimes, Weather is weather, Company News is company news. Some, such as Briefcase, are not as clear. The full potential of many content modules is not immediately obvious. The pop-up window that appears when you click on an entry on the Add Content page doesn't always convey what that module can do for you. Therefore, you'll find more detailed descriptions of many of the more important ones, along with some possible applications, in the following sections. Some features, such as Yahoo!'s Calendar, require several paragraphs to point out the possibilities, some require just a sentence. Some are stand-alone features, in that you can get to them directly rather than going through My Yahoo!, and some—Health News, for example—are also accessible from more than one point within

Yahoo!. Often, placing a module on your My Yahoo! page simply provides a convenient gateway into the corresponding section of Yahoo!, such as Yahoo! Movies, TV, Sports, or News.

The descriptions that follow represent some of the most popular and/or most interesting of the modules. They are arranged here by the category in which you will find them in that category's "Most Popular" list; however if you don't find what you are looking for as you browse, try typing the name of the module into the Find box. Keep in mind that many or most modules can be found listed in multiple categories. As well, watch out for modules coming and going, for inconsistency in the documentation when changes are made, and also for variations in terminology. Selections from the Yahoo! Services are discussed first. The Editors' Picks and Popular from the Web categories are described next, followed by the selections (listed in alphabetic order) from each of the 13 subject-specific categories that appear on the main Add Content page (see Figure 3.3).

Yahoo! Services

The Yahoo! Services category includes some of the most basic and widely useful Yahoo! offerings. As is true throughout the Add Content pages, most of these modules will also be found listed in other categories.

Weather

The Weather module provides current weather conditions for cities you select. The page shows the high and low temperature forecast for the day, along with a link to the full weather report for each city. You can enter a ZIP code or city name to get the weather for other U.S. locations. For non-U.S. cities, enter the name and country: Paris, France, for example. To select cities for your My Yahoo! Weather module, click the Edit button. The next page lets you search for specific locations or browse a regional listing. You can also choose whether to display temperatures in Fahrenheit or

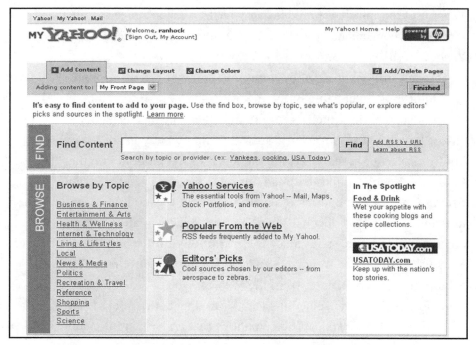

Figure 3.3 My Yahoo! Add Content Page

Celsius. Weather information is provided by the Weather Channel (weather.com). See Chapter 9, Other Seriously Useful Yahoo! Stuff, for more details on Yahoo! Weather.

Message Center

This option places a module on your page with links to Yahoo! Mail, Calendar, and other tools. You can edit the module to check Messenger for friends online, compose e-mail, and view your Calendar, Address Book, Notepad, and Briefcase.

Stock Portfolios

Dozens, if not hundreds, of Web sites offer stock quotes, investment news, and related services, such as tracking your own portfolio. Most such sites provide at least basic information such as current prices, volume, ranges, and ratios. How much information you need depends on how "into" investing you are. Many people find that

Yahoo!'s Portfolio option is more than adequate for your needs. With it, you can choose which stocks, mutual funds, and market indices, both U.S. and non-U.S., you want to follow. You can create as many Yahoo! portfolios as you want and track your own holdings, including their total value, value change, gain or loss, and so on. As on many other investment sites, quotes are delayed by 15 or 20 minutes. Real-time quotes are available as a Premium service.

The Portfolio module has two different Edit options. The standard Edit button in the top border lets you change or delete any of your current portfolios as well as creating new ones. You can also sort the order in which your portfolios are displayed. The Edit link next to the name of a specific portfolio allows you to add or delete symbols and change the display in your My Yahoo! module. Clicking on the name of a portfolio gives you full details about its contents, and clicking on a ticker symbol within a portfolio gives details about the stock, mutual fund, or index. For more information on portfolios, see Chapter 9.

TV Listings

With the TV Listings module, you can view programming for your selection of channels (up to 60). Use the Edit button to identify your TV service providers from lists of cable and satellite systems and over-the-air broadcasters, or choose nationwide listings by time zone. (The initial listings you get are based on the ZIP code in your Yahoo! Profile.) Then choose the stations you want to see, how many (15, 30, 54, all) to display in the module, and the default programming beginning time—that is, which two-hour time slot to show first.

From the listings shown in your module, click on the title of the program to see details, for instance, which Masterpiece Theatre episode is showing today, with a brief description of the episode and the cast. The program description pages include a link to add the program to your Yahoo! Calendar.

Both the program description page and your My Yahoo! module let you search program titles for a particular program. The Advanced Search link permits you to search by program title, subtitle, keywords, cast/crew, and date range, and to sort search results chronologically or by relevance. The TV listings content is drawn from Yahoo! TV, which you can access directly at tv.yahoo.com.

For *severely* serious searchers who may feel guilty about taking advantage of the "entertainment" side of Yahoo!, be aware that this module, especially the search function, is a good way to research what programs are coming up on topics of redeeming educational and professional interest. Got that?

Movie Showtimes

The Movie Showtimes module provides a really easy way to find what movies are showing in your neighborhood, where, and when. It is also a convenient gateway into Yahoo!'s extensive Movies section. The initial list of theaters you see in the module is based on the geographic area indicated in your Yahoo! Profile. Add or change locations using the "City & State or Zip" search box on the module's Edit page. Then click on the list of "Available Theaters" and choose the ones you want to appear in your module. You can also search for a specific movie or theater.

For each theater you select, your My Yahoo! module displays the address, movies currently showing, and showtimes. Click on the name of a theater for a showtimes page with more details about the theater. Use the date box on that page to see what movies are coming up in the next few days. Click on the name of a movie for extensive information including a detailed description, ratings, cast and credits, and reviews. Click on a name in the cast/credits section to see what other movies they have worked on. Many movie listings also include a link to a video trailer.

You can even buy tickets online. From your Movies module, click on a specific showtime to access Fandango, a Yahoo! partner through which you can purchase tickets for many, though not all, theaters.

The Yahoo! Movies page (movies.yahoo.com) includes articles, reviews, trailers and clips, photos, message boards, and other links to take you even further into movieland.

Calendar

The Calendar module, as it appears on your My Yahoo! page, shows events for the next few days that you've added to the Calendar, plus a small calendar for the current month with each day linked to your calendar entries for that day. However, the Yahoo! Calendar can do a lot more for you than simply list your appointments. You can access it (as well as the rest of your My Yahoo! page) from virtually any computer in the world that's connected to the Internet. Others can also access it from anywhere, if you've set it up that way, which makes the calendar a great collaboration tool. The calendar allows you to send reminders to yourself of upcoming events and tasks. You can also list and print calendar pages, events, and tasks in a variety of ways, synchronize the calendar with your Palm Desktop and with Outlook, and do a variety of other useful things. You can get to the calendar directly at calendar.yahoo.com, from the Calendar link on the Yahoo! home page, from your Yahoo! Messenger window, or via a button on the Yahoo! Companion Toolbar. From the Toolbar, it takes just one click to get to the calendar; the arrow to the right of the button lets you choose the display and add items to your Calendar.

The real power of many My Yahoo! modules is revealed once you click the Edit button. The Calendar's Edit button allows you to specify how many days' worth of events to show (up to seven), and the placement of the month calendar relative to the daily event listings. You can also protect your privacy by choosing, on the Edit screen, not to display events unless you've recently entered your password. But the Calendar's *real* power becomes apparent when you go one or two clicks deeper and start adding events. To see what the

Calendar can really do, click on any date and select "Month" for the monthly view of the calendar (see Figure 3.4). Here you begin—just *begin*—to see the Calendar's easy navigability and large number of useful features. The right and left arrows next to the name of the month allow you to move to the next or previous month. Each day includes an "Add" link and the titles of any events you have added to that day. Tabs above the calendar let you change the view to day, week, or month, or list by event or task. Toward the top of the screen are tabs that take you to Yahoo! Mail, Addresses, and Notepad. Each Calendar view includes a search box for events and, below the search box, an Advanced Search to limit your search by type of event and to title or notes. Each view also includes links labeled Sharing, Sync, and Calendar Options. I'll describe these and other tools shortly. As you examine the Calendar features, keep in mind the "collaborative" opportunities they provide, as well as the strictly "personal."

Add Event

The Add Event page starts with a Title box where you can enter up to 80 characters to identify the event in various calendar views. Most of the other information that you enter about the event appears when you click on the title. A pull-down window allows you to slot each event into any of 28 categories, such as Appointment, Class, and Dinner. You can use these categories later to sort your Events list by type of event. The date section of the Add Event page lets you choose any date by clicking the calendar icon to the right of the date windows. A month calendar pops up so you can see the context and identify free times. The time section of the Add Event page allows you to identify the event as "all day" or to specify a start time and duration. A Location box permits you to show the location of the event if you wish, and a Notes box lets you add up to 120 characters of information about the event. There's also a space to enter a related address and phone number.

Figure 3.4 Monthly Calendar View

A Sharing option allows you to tag the event as Private, Public, or "Shows as Busy" (more about sharing shortly). The Repeating area of the Add Event page is where you indicate recurring events, and their frequency and duration. If you indicate, for instance, that an event takes place every second Monday for the next two years, it is automatically added to your calendar for each of those dates. The Invitations section of the Add Events page allows you to notify others about the event. See the section called Inviting Others to an Event.

In the Reminders portion of the Add Events page, you can specify that Yahoo! send you one or two reminders, anywhere from 15 minutes to two weeks before the event, to your regular or mobile device e-mail address or via Yahoo! Messenger. To set default Reminder options, go to the Reminders section of the Calendar Options page.

The Repeating, Invitations, and Reminders sections of the Add Event page include Hide/Show toggles. If you don't see the options you expect for a particular section, click on the Show link. You may prefer to hide any that you don't use very often.

Add Task

This option allows you to add to your calendar tasks that are not associated with a particular day, but show in a separate box in all views. On the Add Task screen you assign a title to the task, add notes if you want, and specify a due date if any, a priority (1–5), and whether the task is to be shared (Public or Private).

Calendar Options

You'll find this link on any calendar page. Calendar Options lets you set a wide assortment of display options, as well as whether you want your calendar sent to you daily via e-mail, where and when to send reminders of specific events, whether to share your calendar and with whom, and more.

Events and Tasks Listings

You can opt to list scheduled events and tasks by type instead of in calendar style. Both lists are sortable. The checkboxes next to each item let you easily delete selected items. The "Show Type" window at both the top and the bottom of the Events list enables you to view just a particular category of event. Both Events and Tasks lists offer a "Quick Add" box for adding new items.

Sharing

The Sharing option is a major feature that greatly expands the potential usefulness of Yahoo!'s Calendar. When you make your calendar "Public" rather than "Private," friends, colleagues, committee members, and others can view it and even modify it if you set it up that way. Click on Sharing on any page of your calendar to display your options. You can add a calendar's URL to an organization's

Web site so that anyone with access to that Web site can get to the calendar. You can even control the degree of access at the individual event level. You can mark some events as private and share others with anyone or with selected people. The options for sharing are:

- "No one can view my calendar" (actually, you still can)
- "Friends can view my calendar; Special Friends can also modify my calendar"
- "Anyone can view my calendar"
- "Anyone can view my calendar; Special Friends can also modify my calendar"

"Anyone" indeed means *anyone*. A Yahoo! ID is not required. "Friends" and "Special Friends," however, must have Yahoo! IDs. You can enter a list of Friends, add or delete names, and grant "Special" status by choosing "View/Modify Events" for selected Yahoo! IDs. Once you elect to share your calendar, others can easily get to it by typing its URL in their browser. The URL is calendar.yahoo.com/ followed by your Yahoo! ID.

The second section on the Sharing options page lets you set the default for your calendar events as "Private," "Show as Busy," or "Public." All events will carry the same default unless you specify otherwise when you add a particular event. "Private" means that only you can see it; "Show as busy" means that others can see that you have an event scheduled, but no further details; "Public" means that others can also view the details.

Inviting Others to an Event

There are a couple of ways to send invitations to an event. Click on its title in any of your calendar views, and the Edit Event page asks "Want to tell others about this event?" In that section you will find a (very long) URL that you can copy and paste into an e-mail message. If your recipients use a Yahoo! Calendar and receive their e-mail in HTML format, all they have to do is click on the URL in the e-mail message to automatically add the event to *their* calendar.

Alternatively, when you initially create an event, you can enter e-mail addresses in the Invitations section of the Add Event page. Then, when you click "Save," or "Save and add another," you'll see a "Notify Your Guests about...." page. Here you can request an RSVP or an e-mail message when the guest responds, or send an e-mail with an "Add to My Calendar" link. You can enter recipients' addresses or Yahoo! IDs in the "To" box, insert addresses from your Yahoo! Address Book, or invite a Yahoo! Group. Information about the host, date, and time will be sent automatically, and you can add a message to accompany the invitation.

After you send out the invitation, your Event page will include a "View Invite" link that shows who has accepted, declined, and not responded. You can issue additional invitations by clicking on the event link on your calendar and entering more names in the Invitations section.

Time Guides

This function allows you to automatically add a variety of events to your calendar, including financial events for stocks listed in your Yahoo! portfolio, events on friends' calendars, Yahoo! Group calendar events, holidays, and sports schedules. To add any of these, click Calendar Options and then the Time Guides link. You can select various calendar display options for each event source. The Time Guide events will appear with a different color background than your own events.

Synchronizing

Downloading a paid version of the Intellisync software enables you to synchronize your Yahoo! Calendar, Address Book, and Notepad with Outlook, Outlook Express, Palm OS handhelds, Lotus Organizer, and ACT!. Follow the instructions under the Sync link on any Calendar view page.

Import and Export

The Import and Export feature lets you export your Yahoo! Calendar data to your Palm Desktop or to Outlook, and vice versa.

Printable View

Click this link for a printable version of the calendar that's much neater than what you'd get by just printing the contents of the browser window.

Explore the calendar to find even more useful features. Its possibilities go far beyond what you see at first glance.

Yahoo! Mail Preview

Adding Mail Preview to your page gives you a preview of messages waiting in your Yahoo! Mail Inbox by showing sender, date, and subject. The Edit button permits you to specify how many messages (from one to nine) to display. You can also instruct the module to show mail messages only if you have recently entered your password. This protects your e-mail from curious eyes should you leave My Yahoo! on your screen while you are away from your computer.

The Yahoo! Mail Preview box shows you exactly when the message list was last updated and provides a link to refresh the list. Other links let you display the complete Inbox and compose a new message. This module allows immediate and easy access to your Yahoo! Mail without having to open a separate browser window. (See Chapter 6, Yahoo!, The Great Communicator, for details on Yahoo! Mail.)

Yellow Pages

The Yellow Pages module lets you search for a specific business (e.g., Wal-Mart) or a category of business (e.g., hardware) in or near a selected location. Results display, by default, for the ZIP code in your Yahoo! profile. You can establish up to five additional locations by using the Edit button. Once you have added locations, a pull-down window allows you to limit your search to any one.

Bookmarks

The Bookmarks module gives you access to your favorite Web sites no matter what computer you're on. The simplest way to add a bookmark is to click the "Add" link next to the "My Bookmarks" title in the module. On the resulting page, enter the URL, a name for the site, and a comment if you want; then click "Save" or "Save and Add Another."

You can also import and export bookmarks or arrange your bookmarks in different folders. "Import Bookmarks" enables you to copy your existing bookmarks from Internet Explorer. If that doesn't work, try the link for manually importing bookmarks. That link leads to the Microsoft program for saving bookmarks as a file that you can then import into Yahoo!. "Export bookmarks" lets you save your My Yahoo! bookmarks as an HTML file that can be opened and used in any browser. "New Folder" allows you to create additional folders in which to arrange your bookmarks.

When doing a Web search in Yahoo!, you can right-click and choose "Add this link to my Yahoo! bookmarks." The link will appear in your "My Bookmarks" folder. To move it to another folder, click on "My Bookmarks," check the appropriate box, and use the "Move to" button to make the transfer. Your My Yahoo! Bookmarks module can handle up to a thousand bookmarks and folders (combined).

Phone Search

The Phone Search module comes in handy for quick lookups of an individual's phone number or address in the U.S. You can search by first name, last name (required), city, and state. Results come from Yahoo! People Search (people.yahoo.com), which takes its information from published phone directories. On Phone Search results pages, you can create, edit, or delete your own listing in Yahoo!'s phone directory database.

Lottery Results

Never again forfeit that $50 million lottery prize because you forgot to check the winning numbers. The Lottery Results module provides winning lottery numbers by U.S. state. Use the Edit button to specify the states you want to display. The "Full Results and Payouts" link leads to detailed information for each lottery, including winning numbers, jackpot, next play, next jackpot, and past results.

Address Book

The Address Book module permits you to store phone numbers, addresses, and related information. You can use the Address Book for quick lookups, or in conjunction with your Yahoo! Mail, Groups, and Calendar, as well as elsewhere. Even if you have other address books, consider using Yahoo!'s as a backup, or as your "traveling" address book. It lets you access needed information from anywhere you have an Internet connection. You can input information manually, gather it from Yahoo! Mail messages you have sent and received, or import it from Outlook Express, Outlook, Palm Desktop, or Netscape Address Book.

To get started with the Address Book, click on the "View All" link. You can add contact information using the "Add Contact," "Quick Add Contact," or "QuickBuilder" link. "Quick Add" lets you enter basic data: first and last name, e-mail, a home, work, or mobile phone number, and a nickname. QuickBuilder enables you to add contacts automatically from your Yahoo! E-mail. You can be more selective by limiting the input to addresses that have appeared two, three, or four times in one, three, six, or twelve months.

"Add Contact" allows you to add alternate e-mail addresses, additional phone numbers (home, work, mobile, pager, fax, other), home address, personal Web site, company information, birthday, anniversary, and notes. You can add up to four fields of your own using the "Edit Custom Fields" section under "Addresses Options" on the main page. You can also assign the contact to a category of your own choosing, such as Commercial, Personal, or Professional. The Address book comes with some pre-assigned category names, but you can add, delete, or edit categories via the Edit button on the category list. If you have added a number of contacts and later want to move them to a category, you can do it easily from the list of names. Click the checkboxes for the entries you want to move, then select "Move to Category" to select the category and move the checked entries.

As with other e-mail address books, you can use set up mailing lists to send a message to a group of people at once. The "Add List" link on the Yahoo! Address Book more precisely means *create* a list. Name the list, then add contacts, either individually from the window that shows your current contacts, or by adding a whole category or everyone in your address book. A list can contain up to a hundred people.

You can access your contact information from the Address Book module on your My Yahoo! page, from your Yahoo! e-mail account, or from the Companion Toolbar. From the Address book, you can see all contacts by using the "View All" link, or browse a portion of the alphabet by clicking on the letter. A search box allows you to search for contacts by first name, last name, nickname, or e-mail domain. When viewing a list of names, you can sort by first name, last name, or e-mail by using the links at the top right of the list.

The "Address Book Options" link allows you not only to create custom fields, but also to set the number of contacts displayed by page and a default category to display. It also lets you edit categories, create a printable version of the entire address book or a specific category, import or export addresses, or synchronize the Yahoo! Address Book with Outlook, Outlook Express, Palm OS handhelds, Lotus Organizer, and ACT!.

The Address Book is one of several My Yahoo! modules that helps provide a personal virtual office wherever you are.

E-Mail Search

The E-Mail Search module allows you to search for e-mail addresses from your My Yahoo! page. Don't expect too much. (Why is it that 3,000 former government leaders in Nigeria know my e-mail address, but most e-mail search tools can't find it?) You can search by combinations of last name, first name, and domain. The Advanced link lets you search by geographic area, organization name or type, and old or last-known e-mail address. If you discover that your own entry is missing or wrong, you can add or correct it using the "Edit/Create My Listing" link.

Package Tracker

The Package Tracker module lets you track packages in transit with Airborne Express, Federal Express, UPS, or the U.S. Postal Service. Click on the link for the shipper you want, then on the following page, enter the tracking number.

Briefcase

The Briefcase module is based on the idea of being able to carry your files with you wherever you go. The Briefcase module stores them for you on the Yahoo! site so you can access them from just about anywhere. The Briefcase is a useful "just in case" when you're traveling. It also provides offsite backup and an easy way to transfer files from one computer to another. Just upload your files to the Briefcase and pick them up from your new location or computer. You can also use the Briefcase to share files with friends and colleagues.

The first time you use your Briefcase you're asked to specify the default sort order for your files: name, type, size, or date, and ascending or descending order. Then you can add files, manage your folders, and share selected folders with your friends. Yahoo! gives you a rather impressive 30 megabytes of storage for free, enough for about 10,000 pages of text. Both the Briefcase page and the corresponding module on your My Yahoo! page display the percentage of your storage quota that you've used.

In many modules the Edit button is where things happen, but in the Briefcase module it's the Add Files link. That's the starting point not only for uploading files to your Briefcase, but for creating and deleting files and folders, and viewing folder contents. From the Briefcase page, the "Add Files" link takes you to the "Select Folders" page. There you can choose a current folder or create a new one for the files you want to upload. A "Browse" button lets you select the files on your computer to upload. You can rename the uploaded file if you want. Yahoo! lets you upload five files at a time, but a single upload cannot exceed 5 MB. If you pay for Premium Service, you can upload 15MB at a time, as well as increase your total storage quota.

The "Share with Friends" feature allows you to specify the Yahoo! IDs of people you're allowing to view the files in a particular folder. You can enter their IDs manually or insert them from your Yahoo! Address Book. You can also limit access to Yahoo! members older than 18. Sharing with the public at large, including those poor souls without Yahoo! IDs, is available as a Premium Service.

The Briefcase module on your My Yahoo! page displays the folders in your Briefcase. To see the files within a folder, click the little arrow next to the folder name. Your Briefcase can be accessed directly at briefcase.yahoo.com/*yourYahooID*. If you're logged in to Yahoo! already, you don't need to type the ID.

HotJobs

The HotJobs module comes from HotJobs, Yahoo!'s employment database. With HotJobs you can create a resume using an easy step-by-step process, run saved job searches ("agents") you have set up, see a list of "Hottest Jobs in My Area," or do a job search in the HotJobs database by keyword, city, and state. The Edit button allows you to choose which of these options appear in your module and to narrow by location and industry the job listings that appear in your "Hottest Jobs" list.

Bill Pay

The Bill Pay module is identical to the Bill Pay option on Yahoo!'s Finance page. The feature is similar to online bill payment services available through your own bank and elsewhere. The Basic plan, which is free, lets you make payments online to more than 100 billers. The Premium plan covers more than 200 billers. If a biller is on Yahoo!'s list, you can view not only the numbers, but also an image of the bill itself. You can add billers that are not on the list. Bill Pay can also send e-mail reminders when bills are due, schedule automatic payments, project your cash flow, and review your payment histories.

Popular from the Web and Editors' Picks

The categories Popular From the Web and Editors' Picks contain "hand-picked" RSS feeds and the lists may change frequently. Some of the sites are very well-known news sites, such as BBC and New York Times. Others are a bit more esoteric, such as Braingle ("brain teasers, mind puzzles and riddles") and Awful Plastic Surgery ("a chronicle of celebrity plastic surgery"). The modules listed in these two categories are useful for identifying some fun sites and also sites that a lot of people should be aware of. If you are looking for specific news site modules, instead of these categories, you will probably want to start with the News & Media category on the Add Content page.

Business & Finance

The Business & Finance modules provide a variety of tools and resources associated with—you guessed it—business and finance (see Figure 3.5). Most relate to investing, and also appear on the Yahoo! Finance page. The modules in the Personal Finance subcategory include options for automatic bill paying, transferring money, monitoring auto loan and mortgage rates, consolidating information about your bank and credit card accounts, and articles on related topics. All items in this category are also found on Yahoo!'s Finance page (finance.yahoo.com), which is discussed in Chapter 8, Yahoo! Finance.

Market Summary

The Market Summary module provides a quick look at the current quotes and day's change for the major U.S. markets and indices. Click Edit to change which indices are displayed, to add a chart for one or more of the indices, and to add a brief summary paragraph describing current market conditions.

Company News

The Company News module provides headlines about stocks or mutual funds that you have included in your Yahoo! Portfolios.

Figure 3.5 Business & Finance Category Choices

Click on the headline to go to the full story on a Yahoo! Finance page. News stories originate with Yahoo! News providers, such as PrimeZone Media Network, PR Newswire, and CBS MarketWatch. The module's Edit button allows you to delete news coverage for any of your ticker symbols, and to specify which news sources you want, how far back to go, and how many headlines (up to 10) per company to display.

Currency Converter

For international travelers especially, the Currency Converter is a very handy tool for keeping up on changes or calculating the conversion value for a particular sum. The "Convert" window allows you to specify an amount and convert from and to any of more than 150 currencies. The "answer" takes the form of a Yahoo! Finance page that gives you not just the amount, but charts showing recent changes, a table comparing exchange rates for major currencies, and links to recent news stories relating to currencies. The Currency Converter module on your My Yahoo! page displays a comparative chart of currencies and their values. The Edit button allows you to specify which currencies to display.

Stock Upgrades & Downgrades

The Upgrades & Downgrades module reports recent changes in analysts' ratings of particular securities. The data from major analysts is provided by Briefing.com. The information appears under the headings Upgrades, Downgrades, and Initiated. Clicking on any of these headings takes you to the Yahoo! Finance Analyst Recommendations page, which offers many links to historical and current news and statistics about the securities in question.

Mortgage Monitor

The Mortgage Monitor lets you follow rates in one or two states that you select via the Edit button. It displays average rate, points, and APR for 30-year fixed, 15-year fixed, and ARM mortgages. You can also opt to see national averages.

Earnings Surprises

The Earnings Surprises module displays surprises for the day from Quarterly Earnings Reports, broken down into Upsides and Downsides. Each listing shows Earnings Per Share and percentage surprise. Clicking on either Upsides or Downsides yields the Yahoo! Finance - Quarterly Earnings Surprises page, with links to further information for the securities listed.

SmartMoney.com Personal Finance

The SmartMoney.com Personal Finance module provides links to featured articles on personal finance from the SmartMoney.com site.

Entertainment & Arts

All work modules and no play modules make for either a dull My Yahoo! page or a more productive one. Your call.

Comics

The Edit button on the Comics module lets you choose up to three cartoons from a list of more than 50 funnies and editorial cartoons and place them on your My Yahoo! page.

Movie Releases

The Movie Releases module focuses on current releases. Clicking on the name of a movie takes you to its page in the Yahoo! Movies section. The module's Edit button lets you display lists of new and upcoming releases, as well as weekend and daily top box office.

New on DVD

You guessed it—this module lists new DVD releases. Click on a link and you go to the Yahoo! Shopping page for that item. Most

Popular DVDs and New DVD Releases—Rock and Pop are other DVD modules you can add.

Health & Wellness

Most of the Health & Wellness modules provide a feature story or tip on a particular aspect of health.

Ask the Doctor

The Ask the Doctor module produces advice from "Natural Health Advice from Dr. Andrew Weil" and "Children's Health Advice from Dr. Greene." Use the Edit button to choose one or both.

General Health Tip

Adding this module will deliver one or two tips a day to your My Yahoo! page. The tips come from Yahoo!'s Daily Tips or Health sections.

Back Care Center

This module provides tips and general information related to the back and its care. Information comes from Back.com, iScoliosis.com, and NeckReference.com

Allergy Watch

The Allergy Watch module provides allergy-related headlines from Yahoo!'s Health section, plus a pollen count for the U.S. city of your choice from Accuweather.com. Select your city using the Edit button.

Diet Tracker

Enter Start Date, End Date, and End Weight (goal), then periodically use either the Edit button or the "Weigh-In" link to enter your current weight. Diet Tracker provides you with a bar graph and percentage showing your progress.

Asthma Watch

Use the Asthma Watch module to get asthma news headlines from Yahoo!'s Health section and a link to Today's Air Quality for a U.S. city of your choice from Accuweather.com. The Edit button lets you choose your city.

Clinical Trials

The Clinical Trials Module allows you to track clinical trials by U.S. state and disease or condition. To see the information, you must register (free) with the provider of the information, Acurian. Use the Edit button to enter a location and choose from more than 50 diseases and conditions.

Pregnancy Calendar

Use the Edit button to enter basic dates and data. The Pregnancy Calendar details the probable growth of the baby.

Internet & Technology

This category provides an interesting and varied assortment of Internet and technology-related content, including search, news, and tools. You will find the modules related to Yahoo's search function (Search, Saved Searches, Buzz Index) under the Web Search sub-category here.

Yahoo! Search

This module contains the Yahoo! Search box. With it on your page, you can do a Yahoo! search by entering search terms here in the same way you would enter them in the Search box on Yahoo!'s main page or on the search.yahoo.com page. For details on searching Yahoo!, see Chapter 2, Searching and Browsing the Web with Yahoo!.

Saved Searches

If you run particular Web searches frequently, or want to *remember* to run them frequently, you can store them in the Saved Searches module. Use the Edit button to create new searches and edit or delete existing ones. Once you've set up a search, just click on it in the module to run it via Yahoo!'s Web search engine.

When setting up a search this way, you use basically the same techniques as for a regular Yahoo! Web search: Multiple words are automatically ANDed; use an "OR" between terms if any (or all) of them can appear in your results; enclose phrases in quotation marks. You can also use prefixes such as "intitle:". An Advanced Search link allows you to structure a search using the features on the Yahoo! Search advanced search page. See Chapter 2 for lots more on searching the Web with Yahoo!.

The Saved Searches module is also useful if you regularly run a search in which a portion changes. You can set up the basic query as a saved search, then modify it, once you have a results page in front of you, by adding additional terms in the search box.

Buzz Index

Ever curious about what other people are searching on Yahoo!? That's what the Buzz Index is all about. This module provides a ranking of the most popular search topics in terms of "Leaders" and "Movers." Leaders are the most popular in a given week. Movers are the ones with the greatest percentage increase in their score. The score is based on the percentage of total Yahoo! searches that a particular topic accounted for, multiplied by a constant. Click on any link in the box to get extensive detail. The Edit button allows you to investigate leaders and movers in the following categories: Overall, Television, Music, Sports, and Movies. In addition to the curiosity factor, the Buzz Index might be useful for marketing and competitive intelligence purposes.

Notepad

The Notepad is another module that can help make My Yahoo! an integral part of your virtual office (see Figure 3.6). Use the Notepad to write reminders to yourself, drafts of letters, lists, or anything else you'd jot down in a paper notepad. Your notepad will be available to you via the Internet wherever you are.

Your My Yahoo! screen displays a list of your notes along with a "New Note" box. Just type a note in the box and click "Save." The first line of your note becomes the title of the note. A note can be quite lengthy—up to 5,000 characters.

Click on the title of any note to see the full text. At this point, you can edit the text, delete it, click "Printable View" to get a printer-friendly version, or file it in a folder. After you click Update, Delete, or Cancel, Yahoo! returns you to your main Notebook page, which lists all your notes by name, the folders they're in, and when they were last modified. Click on any of these to sort the list by that criterion. Checkboxes next to the note titles allow you to delete several notes at a time. You can also click on a folder to see its contents, or use the "Add folder" button to create a new folder. A Search box

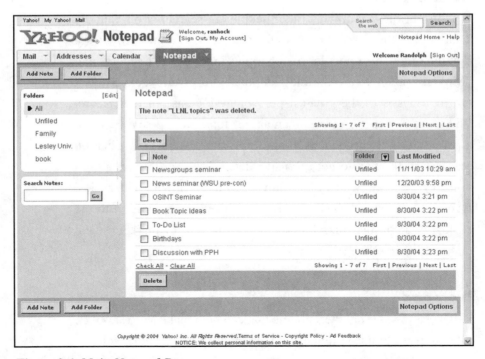

Figure 3.6 Main Notepad Page

allows you to search all your notes for specific content. If you enter multiple words, they'll be searched as a phrase.

The Edit button on the Notepad module allows you to set the number of note titles to be displayed (from 1 to 10) as well as the placement of the Add Note box. It also gives you the option to not display notes on your My Yahoo! page unless you entered your password recently.

A Notepad tab appears on Yahoo! Mail, Calendar, and Address Book screens, making it easy to access from any of those tools. You can also access it directly from notepad.yahoo.com/*yourYahooID*, or just notepad.yahoo.com if you're already signed in to Yahoo!.

Domain Search

This module lets you search for available Web domain names. If the name is already taken, it suggests other possible names and domains. You can also purchase domains through Yahoo!.

Mobile Downloads

The Mobile Downloads module provides downloadable (for a fee) applications for Palm OS, Pocket PC, Windows CE, and Symbian/EPOC. Choose your device via the Edit button, then select from "What's New," "Popular," "Best Sellers," or "Downloads of the Day."

Inside My Yahoo!

Inside My Yahoo! provides tips on using My Yahoo! and alerts you to new modules, new color themes, and other additions and changes to My Yahoo! offerings.

Living & Lifestyles

The modules in this category offer a wide range of living and lifestyle tips and resources.

Horoscopes

Click Edit for your choice of horoscopes—romance, career, etc., and daily, weekly, or monthly—based on the birth date, gender, and astrological signs you specify.

Today's Recipes

The Recipe module provides you with a daily recipe from Yahoo's Health section.

Home Improvement

This module provides brief but useful tips on home improvement and home maintenance from ServiceMagic.

Deals of the Day

This module shows featured "deals" in selected consumer product categories. You can choose up to seven using the Edit button. Click on a product name to get details. Click on the category name, such as Computers and Electronics, or the "More great deals" link, to see more products from the seller of the featured item.

Local

The Local section of modules primarily contains news, weather, and sports sources, arranged from a geographic (city, region, country) perspective. Modules for Yahoo!'s very informative and useful City Guides are also located here. For a feel for the full range of news, see the News section itself.

City Guides

The City Guides module gives you quick access to your choice (up to three) of the approximately 100 Yahoo! U.S. City Guides. Use the Edit button to select cities. Each guide includes links to restaurant or other reviews and a calendar of events. You can search by city, state, or ZIP code to find the equivalent information in other City Guides. See Chapter 9 for more about Yahoo! City Guides.

News & Media

This section contains more than 200,000 news sources, ranging from international sources to hometown sources and from traditional sources such as Reuters to new sources such as Weblogs. You will want to explore the subcategories, but also make use of the search box to find local and specialized news. Once you have added a news module to your page, you can click on the Edit button for the module to specify that from one to 10 headlines be displayed and to specify the date range to be displayed (1–6 days).

Much of the news content is available thanks to RSS technology. RSS stands for "Really Simple Syndication" and is a format by which news providers large and small can easily distribute their content. Using RSS, Yahoo! can gather headlines from your choice of sources and display them as links on your My Yahoo! page. This means that, in addition to headlines from Yahoo! News providers, such as Reuters and AP, you can choose from thousands of other news sources that provide an RSS format. An increasing number of news sites feature "Add to My Yahoo!" RSS links. Just click the link and the RSS feed is added. This is definitely one of the easiest ways to take advantage of RSS resources.

Reuters Top Stories

This module delivers top stories, continually updated, from what is considered by many to be the world's leading news wire service.

News Photos

The News Photos module provides a selection of current news photographs. The Edit button lets you choose one or more of the following categories: Most Viewed Photos, Most E-mailed Photos, Most Viewed Slideshows, and Entertainment Photos, as well as the number of photos (1–5) to display for each category you choose.

USA Today: Top Stories

Top stories from a leading national newspaper.

News Clipper

The News Clipper module provides a way to quickly check Yahoo! News for current stories on any topic of interest to you.

To use it, set up a search query, give it a name, then run it whenever you wish by clicking on the name in the News Clipper module. Use the Edit button to create new searches, and to edit or delete existing searches. When creating or editing a search, a pull-down window next to the search box allows you to specify "Matches on any word," "Matches all words," or "An exact phrase match." You can also indicate a phrase by enclosing it in quotation marks. Other windows let you limit your retrieval to the last day, three days, week, or month, sort your results by date or relevance, and display from 1 to 9 stories per search in your News Clipper module.

To keep up-to-date on any topic, also consider using the Alerts feature on the Yahoo! News pages (see Chapter 5, Yahoo! News).

Politics

Many of the sources in the Politics category are from the Politics sections of sources such as Reuters, Associated Press, MSNBC, and washingtonpost.com. You will also find numerous politically oriented Weblogs.

Recreation & Travel

Although most of the modules in this category could be considered as ads for special travel bargains or features, they provide an excellent way of being alerted to some really good deals. Others, such as Maps, provide very handy tools for both the frequent and infrequent traveler.

Maps

If you need a quick map of a U.S. location, the Maps module will provide it. You can specify street address, airport code, city, state, or ZIP code. You can also go back to recent searches via the pull-down window, and add "favorite" locations by using the Edit button.

Results are from Yahoo! - Get Local - Maps. For other things you can do with Yahoo! Maps, see Chapter 9.

Best Fare Tracker

The Edit button here lets you select departure and destination airports for which you want to track airfare bargains. The module displays the lowest round-trip fare on a 21-day purchase. Click on the fare shown for details and availability, and to book your flight through Yahoo! Travel's partner, Travelocity.

Destination Spotlight

Clicking on the city featured in the Destination Spotlight module takes you to that city's Yahoo! Travel page. It includes a slideshow, recommended hotels, restaurants, things to do, shopping, a map, and links to reviews, guides, and airfares. Use the module's search box to check out different destinations.

Travel Deals & Reviews

This module offers travel deals and reviews for featured cities from Concierge.com.

Last-Minute Weekend Getaways

This module features deals on packages for the next two weekends. They include combinations of hotels, rental cars, flights, and so on. Use the Edit button to choose departure cities and price ranges.

American Airlines Specials

Use the Edit button to choose the departure airports you want.

Vacation Specials

This module lists U.S. and Caribbean travel packages. Choose a departure city and a destination by using the Edit button.

Cruise Specials

This module shows you special deals on cruises for the areas (Caribbean, Bahamas, Europe, etc.) that you indicate on its Edit page.

Reference

The reference modules provide a number of handy tools such as fact and phone look-ups, a calculator, Word of the Day, library-related Weblogs, and other tools and resources.

Word of the Day

Putting this module on your page will help assuage any intellectual guilt you might feel for including the TV listings on your My Yahoo! page. The module shows a few synonyms; clicking on "synonyms" leads to more. The "Definition" link leads to a more detailed definition and an audio link to help you with the correct pronunciation. There's also a link to yesterday's word, in case you missed it.

Reference Lookup

If you ever need a quotation, a definition or synonym, or a quick fact about a country or a political or historical figure, keep the Reference Lookup module in mind. A pull-down window allows you to search "All Reference" or to limit your query to the American Heritage Dictionary, Roget's Thesaurus, American Heritage Spanish Dictionary, the Britannica Concise Encyclopedia, Bartlett's Familiar Quotations, Gray's Anatomy, the Oxford Shakespeare, or the World Factbook. Results come from the collection of resources in Yahoo! Education (education.yahoo.com).

Calculator

The Calculator module puts a calculator on your page, on which you can perform the usual arithmetic operations (but nothing fancy like trigonometric functions). You can enter numbers either by clicking on the screen or from your keyboard. (Note: You can do these calculations, and more, right in a Yahoo! Web search box. See Chapter 2.)

Ask Yahoo!

Ask Yahoo! invites users to submit questions on any topic. Yahoo! selects from the questions it receives, researches them, and publishes some of the most interesting ones (along with the answers, of course) on Ask Yahoo!. Click on a question in the Ask Yahoo! module to see the answer. The answer page includes links to most popular questions and previously answered questions in various subject areas.

Science

The Science category, like the Local category, primarily contains news sources. A variety of weather modules for various cities are also found here.

AFP: Science

Agence Press France provides news from the international science community for this module.

Shopping

While the Business & Finance category focuses on how to manage and even increase your net worth, the modules in Yahoo!'s Shopping category encourage you to get rid of all that excess money and do your part to bolster the economy. Chapter 7 goes into more detail about Yahoo!'s various shopping features.

Auctions

The Auctions module lets you track items on the Yahoo! Auction site (auctions.shopping.yahoo.com), whether you're seriously interested, or just keeping an eye on the action. The Edit button lets you customize your module to follow items you're selling, items you're bidding on, your Watchlist, charity auctions, and/or interesting ("Spotlight") auctions. If, for example, you have a bid in on that 1964 Corvair, you'll see it listed in the "Items you are Bidding on" section of the module, with the current bid, high bidder, and time remaining for the auction. The Edit page enables you to display up to nine items in each section.

Best-Selling Books

The Best-Selling Books module provides a list of the top 10 best sellers, including rank, title, and author, from Yahoo!'s shopping site. Click on the title to read reviews, compare prices from various Yahoo! merchants, and buy the book.

Shopping Specials

This feature gives you another opportunity to place ads on your page.

Yahoo! Points

If you have a Yahoo! Visa card, the Yahoo! Points module tracks the points you have earned.

Sports

The Sports modules include Sports Scoreboard, Fantasy Sports, Ski Report, Team Calendars, Team News and individual modules for all major sports. Except for the Ski Report, which comes from Yahoo! Travel (travel.yahoo.com), the content of these modules originates with Yahoo! Sports (sports.yahoo.com).

Scoreboard

The Scoreboard module shows you today's action and yesterday's results for teams in the geographic area indicated in your Yahoo! profile (U.S. only). You can select other teams with the Edit button. You have a choice of professional or NCAA teams. Click on the score or game time in the module to get a game summary. Click on "Scoreboard" to go to the main Yahoo! Sports page. Click on a sports category, such as "MLB" (Major League Baseball), to get to that section of Yahoo! Sports. Click on the team name to see that team's page from Yahoo! Sports.

Fantasy Sports

Own your own team and manage it with the Fantasy Sports module. Click the "Add teams here" link to get started. Use the Edit button to change the order in which your teams appear.

Ski Report

The Ski Report module provides snow reports (new snow and base) for your choice of resorts throughout the U.S., Canada, and seven other countries. Use the Edit button to choose resorts and to specify measurements in inches or centimeters. Click on a resort to see its Yahoo! Travel page, which includes additional details on conditions, links to the resort's Web page, and other ski-related information.

Team Calendars

The Team Calendar module is similar to the Scoreboard module, except that it displays the current week or month's schedule of games for your teams. Click on a team name to see its Yahoo! Sports page. If you click on the game time or the score, you get a preview, summary or recap of the game. The Edit button allows you to choose which teams to display.

MAKING THE BEST USE OF MY YAHOO!

The most important step in getting the most from My Yahoo! is learning which of its multitude of modules particularly interest *you*. Don't forget to explore what the Edit button can do; that's often the key to customizing a particular module to your precise needs.

Finally, remember that as you add modules you can reorganize your My Yahoo! page so that the most important modules, or the ones you use most, are handy. Selecting the modules you can really use, and arranging them optimally on your page, makes a tremendous collection of personally useful data available to you at a glimpse.

CHAPTER 4

Yahoo! Groups

The discussion groups on Yahoo!, also known as Yahoo! Groups, have two distinct benefits. First, they enable anyone to establish and participate in an online meeting place for exchanging information, either with the world at large or with a selected group of people. Secondly, they provide access to a broad database of advice and commentary. You get to Yahoo! Groups by clicking on the Groups link on Yahoo!'s main page, or going directly to groups.Yahoo.com. This chapter explores the range of Yahoo! Group possibilities and how to take advantage of them. It starts with a look at the benefits, then talks about how to find and join groups of interest, how to read and post messages, and a number of additional features that even veteran Yahoo! Group participants might not be aware of.

The first benefit—access to a broad range of advice and commentary—carries with it a set of caveats. That is, the quality of the "advice" will vary greatly, and the "commentary" is likely to range from idiotic babbling to extremely informed and valuable opinion. You'll quickly learn to separate the wheat from the chaff.

The second benefit of Yahoo! Groups is the ability to use it as your own two-way Internet communications channel. You can create a group of your own, or participate in groups created by others, or both. If you want a forum to discuss a particular topic, or an electronic meeting-place for a committee, a class, or family members, you can set up a group in less than five minutes, at no charge. Thousands of trade and professional associations use Yahoo! Groups as their online conference room and as an alternative, hassle-free way to manage their electronic bulletin boards and membership mailing lists. As a bonus, your group can be public or private and include, as you wish, files, photos, links, a database, polls, and a calendar.

Earlier in Internet history, there was a distinct difference between "groups"—including variations such as newsgroups, discussion groups, forums, message boards, and bulletin boards—and "mailing lists." For the former, you *went to* a Web site or a newsgroup reader to read and send messages. For the latter, messages *came to* you via e-mail; you didn't have to "go" anywhere to check or respond to messages. This distinction still exists, but Yahoo! Groups is a hybrid that incorporates features and advantages of both. Members can send and receive messages either by going to the group's Web page on Yahoo! or via e-mail. You don't even have to go to the Web to sign up, if you don't want to. But, as you'll soon see, the offerings and opportunities are much richer if you opt to participate via the Web as opposed to just taking the e-mail route.

The Main Groups Page: Doorway To Yahoo! Groups

The main Yahoo! Groups page, groups.Yahoo.com, consists of three major sections (see Figure 4.1). On the left, you'll see a section labeled either Sign In (if you aren't already signed in) or My Groups, which lists the groups you've joined. Next to it is the heading "What is a Group?," with a link labeled "Start a new Group." Under that, the Join a Group section features a Search box and a directory of Yahoo! groups arranged by category. The Search box gives you direct access to Yahoo!'s tens of thousands of groups, covering topics from politics to pottery, from card games to chemistry. You'll find Yahoo! groups about specific industries, companies, products, software, and almost any other subject you can imagine (including dozens on duct tape). An "Editor's Picks" section highlights "hot" or topical group discussions.

If, heaven forbid, you ignored the advice in Chapter 1 to sign up for a Yahoo! account, now's the time to catch up. Yahoo! Groups are

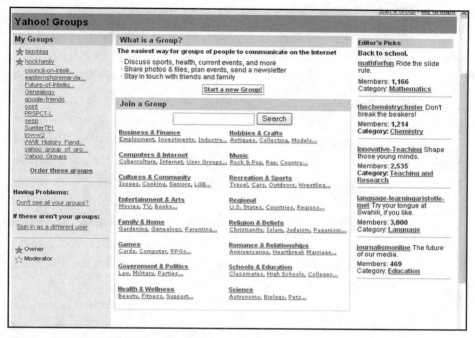

Figure 4.1 Yahoo!'s Main Groups Page

much richer and easier to understand when you're a member. Having done that, try a search on the main Groups page for a topic that particularly interests you. Then go ahead and sign up for one or two groups so you can start to explore what groups are all about. Don't feel that you're committing yourself to a long-term relationship; you can leave a group with just a single click.

CHOOSING A GROUP OF INTEREST
Using the Groups Directory

There are two main ways to locate groups of interest: browsing and searching. The Yahoo! Groups Directory is organized into 16 browseable top-level categories similar but not identical to Yahoo!'s Web directory categories. When you click on a category, you get a link to groups at that level, plus a list of more specialized subcategories. If, for example, you select Science, you see a page with the top section labeled "View Science Groups" containing a link to a listing of the groups that discuss science generally. Underneath that is the header "Browse for More Specialized Groups," with links to subcategories within Science, such as Astronomy, Biology, Chemistry, and Physics.

Clicking on the link under View Science Groups displays a list of groups, a brief description provided by the group "owner," the number of members, and an indication of whether the message archive is public or available to group members only. Knowing the number of members can be especially useful, since more participants might mean more information and expertise available within the group. (Many groups have but a single member. Wouldn't you like to brighten some group owner's day by joining and thereby doubling the membership of his or her group?)

Groups only appear in the directory if the group owner has specified that they be listed there, which means that family or professional groups that are closed to outsiders tend to be "unlisted." Listed groups can be either "public" or members-only. If the former, you can click on the word "public" to read messages from the group. If the latter, you have to join the group before you can look at messages.

On most directory pages and elsewhere in Yahoo! Groups, you'll see Yahoo! Sponsored Links, otherwise known as ads. Instead of resenting their presence, be grateful, since they help underwrite the costs of making this and other Yahoo! features available to you for free. You may even find the ads useful occasionally. That's more likely on the Web than in a newspaper or magazine, since ads you encounter on a Web site are often targeted to your interests.

Using the Groups Search Box

A Search box appears in the Join a Group section on the Groups main page, as well as on directory pages and other locations where it might be useful. Searching is often more effective than the directory for finding groups of interest, particularly if your subject is very specific or does not easily fit in one of the directory categories. Enter one or more words in the search box and you'll get a list of groups that have those words in their name or their description. (The descriptions you see in search results are a bit more extensive than those you get when browsing the directory.) If any of your search terms also appear in category headings, you'll see a list of those matches as well. Be aware that, at this level, you are searching only the group names and descriptions, not the content of messages. You can use the search box from within a specific group to search message content.

Your search query can contain multiple words, but only those records that contain *all* of the words will be retrieved; that is, the words are "ANDed" together. You cannot "OR" terms as you can in a Yahoo! Web search, nor can you use quotation marks to indicate a specific phrase. (Yahoo! will ignore the quotation marks.) See Chapter 2 for more about ANDing and ORing.

Learning More About Yahoo! Groups

Whether you use the directory or the search box to find a group that interests you, clicking on its name, or on the "more" link, takes you to the group's home page (see Figure 4.2). The main components of a group home page are described in the following sections.

Description

The description usually contains an overview of the topical focus of the group, and may contain such information as policies regarding the nature of messages, and restrictions on membership. It also displays the category under which the group is listed, which can be particularly useful for locating similar groups.

Membership Information

Membership Information (or Group Info) lists the number of members in the group, when it was founded, and its language. Group Settings displays a summary of the rules established by the group owner regarding membership, posting of messages, availability of

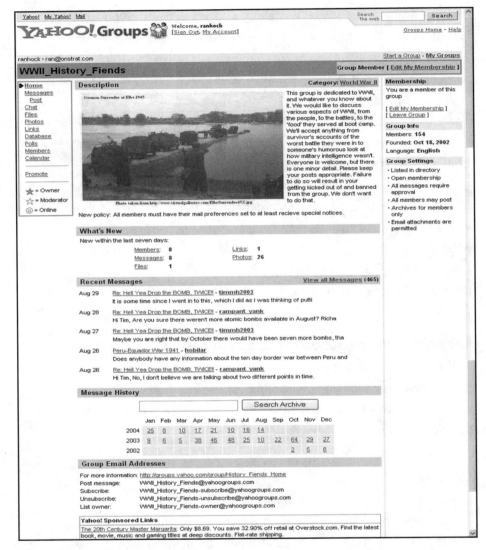

Figure 4.2 Typical Group Home Page

archives, and other features. These settings are discussed below, in
Setting Up a Group. After you join a group, its home page will
include links to edit your various membership options as well as
resign from the group.

Links to Group Features

The left side of a group's home page displays a list of links to messages and other features that the group owner has enabled. These may include chat, files, photos, links, database, polls, members, and calendar. Most of these links only appear as active if you've joined the group.

Messages

Farther down the page, a Recent Messages section lists the last five messages posted to the group, a View All Messages option, and a calendar showing how many messages have been posted each month since the beginning of the group. Clicking on the number in any month will take you to that month's messages.

Group E-Mail Addresses

Toward the bottom of the page is a list of e-mail addresses related to the use of the group, including the e-mail address of the group owner and addresses for posting messages, and subscribing and unsubscribing from the group. You can easily take care of these functions through the Yahoo! Groups pages rather than by e-mail, but their presence here is a reminder that you have that e-mail option.

Search Archives

If the group owner has made the archives public, you'll also find a Search Archives box on this page. This is where you can search the full content of messages that have been posted to the group.

JOINING AND USING A GROUP

When you've found a group that interests you, click on Join This Group to sign up. You'll be asked for your Yahoo! Password. If you *still* don't have a Yahoo! account, you can open one at this point. Then you get to specify the e-mail address you want to use for the group, as well as your e-mail format and delivery preferences. You can opt to receive individual messages as they're posted to the group, or a daily digest of all messages (up to 25 per mailing) posted that day. You can also elect whether to receive special notices or updates from the group's moderator, or no e-mail at all. The latter preference assumes that you'll keep up with messages on the group page instead of in your mailbox. This setting can be useful if you want to temporarily turn off e-mail when you're away from your computer for an extended period.

As part of the group sign-up process, you can create a new profile to use with this group rather than your standard Yahoo! profile. Your group profile might mention something that would interest members of the group, but that you wouldn't necessarily want in your regular profile. Depending on how the group is set up, you may also be able to control unwanted e-mail by hiding your e-mail address from members and/or the moderator. Some groups require that the owner approve all new memberships, and provide a text box for you to enter your reasons for wanting to join. Finally, as a safeguard against automated sign-ups for spamming purposes, you're asked to enter a string of nonsense characters that appears in graphical form at the bottom of the page.

Once you've joined a group, you'll see its name under My Groups on the Yahoo! Groups main page (see Figure 4.1) whenever you're signed in.

Group Owners, Moderators, and Members

As you explore individual groups and perhaps establish a group of your own, you'll notice some "class distinctions." The person who creates a group is its *owner*. He or she, and everyone else who joins the group, are *members*. Especially if a group is large and very active, the owner can share the duties by appointing *moderators*. The most typical task of moderators is to approve messages before posting them for the whole group to read. *Moderated group* generally refers to any group where such approval is required. Groups that don't require such approval are *unmoderated groups*. At the owner's discretion, a Yahoo! group moderator can be empowered to approve or reject messages, invite, add or ban members, change group settings, and perform various other administrative functions. An owner can even appoint additional owners, who have all the powers of the original owner. A blue star beside a name on a list of group members indicates an owner, and a yellow star indicates a moderator.

Viewing Group Messages

Although some groups let anyone read messages simply by clicking the "Public" link next to their group description, chances are you'll be doing most of your reading from the group's home page. Recent messages are listed at the bottom of the page. Click on View all Messages to see a list of all messages, and on the subject header of any message to see its contents (see Figure 4.3). Some groups are used primarily for announcements and therefore don't offer the View all Messages option.

Each message listing includes a column for subject, sender's name or e-mail address, sender's Yahoo! ID, and date posted. Messages are numbered sequentially and displayed in date order. Clicking on the subject takes you to the text of the message. You can click on the sender's name or e-mail address to send a message directly to that person (not to the group). Clicking on the sender's Yahoo! ID shows you their Yahoo! profile.

The Thread link at the top of the message list displays the entire thread for each of the messages. *Thread* refers to the conversational sequence of messages on a topic—the original message, replies to that message, replies to replies, and so on. To read a message thread, click on the first message in the sequence (the one without "RE" preceding the subject). That message will be displayed, along with links to other messages in the thread.

The Expand Messages link displays the complete text of the current page of messages, not just the subject headers.

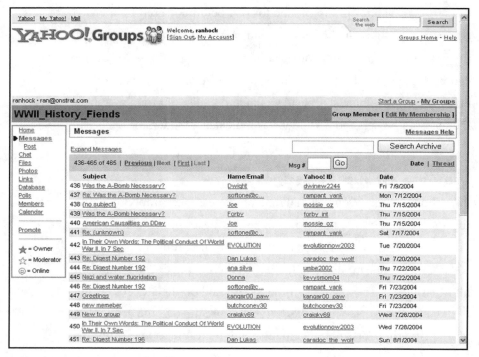

Figure 4.3 "View All Messages" Page

Posting Messages

When reading messages, you have the option to reply to the group. Click Reply, enter your response in the resulting e-mail window, and click Send to share your thoughts with the universe, or a small fraction thereof. If the group is moderated, your message must first be approved by the moderator. Otherwise, it should appear almost immediately on the group's message list. (If you submit a message to a moderated group and it's not approved within 14 days, it will be deleted.)

To start a new message thread on a topic of your choosing, click the Post link that you will find on the left side of the group's home page and elsewhere. Fill in the subject line, enter the text of your message, and click Send. Before you do, though, be aware that your message can be read by all group members and, if it's a public list, by the entire world. Most, but not all, groups limit posting to members of that group.

"My Groups" Page

The groups you've joined are listed for you on the left side of your main Yahoo! Groups page (see Figure 4.1). This is an easy way not only to see your groups but also to get to them quickly. That page also includes a "My Groups" link, which provides a more detailed list of your groups in tabular form, with columns for group name, number of members, your profile and e-mail address for that group, e-mail delivery method, and other settings you've specified. Click a column heading, such as E-mail Address, to sort the list by that criterion. The Edit My Groups link at the top of the page provides a very easy way to change your settings for any or all of your groups.

Additional Yahoo! Group Features

Yahoo! Groups have a great deal of potential value beyond just reading and sending messages. The owner of any group can choose which of the following features to make available and to whom.

Chat

This feature enables you to "chat" in real time with other members of the group. To find someone online to chat with, you can click on the Members link and look for someone with a smiley face icon next to his or her Yahoo! ID. The smiley face icon indicates that that person is online at the moment. Of course, you can also make an appointment, in e-mail or otherwise, to meet someone online for a chat.

Files

If the group moderator has enabled this feature, members can upload files and make them available to others. The files might include, for instance, various forms, reports, spreadsheets, lists, maps, or executable programs. The material you upload must conform to Yahoo!'s Terms of Service (see docs.yahoo.com/ info/terms). Basically, that means nothing illegal, threatening, harassing, defamatory, or so on, may be uploaded. Each group is limited to 20 megabytes for file storage. Other than that, there is no limit to the number of files that can be uploaded, as long as no single file exceeds 5 megabytes. To view and/or upload files, click on the Files link on the group's home page.

Group owners get a number of additional options. They can opt to e-mail a particular text file to group members, for example, when they join or leave the group, or on a regular basis. Plain text files are sent as e-mail messages, other files as attachments. Owners can also choose to notify group members automatically when new items are added to the Files library.

Photos

Up to 30 megabytes of photos can be stored and made available to a group. Click on the Photos link to see photos that have been added. If members are permitted to upload photos, click on Add Photos to contribute yours. The instructions are clearly presented. To add just a few photos, use the Browse and Upload option. To add a large number, use the Upload Tool. This allows you to add captions to pictures and to rotate them if necessary. The Upload Tool is downright nifty. You can arrange photos in albums, rearrange them, and view them as a slideshow.

Links

You can share favorite Web bookmarks with your group, including the URL, name, and description, and organize them in folders. You (or the group's moderator) can also edit or delete the ones you added.

Database

This option lets you upload databases that will display in spreadsheet format. You can create a database from scratch by defining your own fields, or use one of the templates that Yahoo! provides:

Class Assignments, Simple Phone Book, Complete Phonebook, CD Music Library, FAQ, Recipes, Orders, Inventory, and Contact List. Once you have created a database, you can add individual records or import data from another program by saving it in comma, semi-colon, colon, or tab-delimited format, then copying it into the Import box. You can search your database or sort it by any of its fields. You can also specify who within the group is allowed to modify the database in any way. You can export data and print reports for the entire database, or for selected records sorted as you want. The database feature offers a simple yet powerful collaborative working environment for projects and activities.

Polls

With this feature, you can poll members on any topic. Each poll consists of one question, but allows up to 25 options for the answer. When you set up a poll, you specify single vs. multiple answers, whether results will display during the polling or only after the poll is closed, whether the voter's identity is displayed to those who view poll results, when the poll will conclude, and whether results will be sent to the entire group. You can run multiple polls at the same time. All members are notified of the poll via an e-mail message that contains the question, the possible answers, and a link to the poll itself. Past poll results display until the owner or moderator deletes them.

Members

The Members link takes you to the Members page for that group. This page lists all group members with a link to their Yahoo! Profile, their e-mail address, and when they joined the group. Click on the column heading to sort the list by any of those three criteria. The Members page also includes a tab for displaying a list of group moderators, and one that shows "bouncing" members, those whose e-mail addresses may be invalid and whose accounts have been suspended as a result. When e-mail to a member bounces back with an error message, Yahoo! sends a series of test messages. If these messages don't go through, the member's account remains deactivated. If they do go through, the account is reactivated. Bouncing members can reactivate their accounts by going to their "My Groups" page.

Calendar

The calendar not only provides a place for members to learn about and track upcoming events; it's also another very useful collaboration tool. The Calendar works very much like the My Yahoo! calendar described in Chapter 3. You specify the name of the event, the type (for instance, meeting, teleconference, dinner), the start and end times, and add any notes about the event. For recurring events such as monthly meetings, you can set it up so the entry automatically appears on the appropriate date and time. You can also arrange one or two e-mail reminders of upcoming events to be sent to all members at a time you specify, anywhere from two weeks to 15 minutes before the event. You can view the calendar by day, week, month, or year. Tabs take you to a list of events or a list of tasks. All views include a small current-month calendar in which you can click on any date to go to that day's calendar. All views also offer a search box and a link to an Advanced Search capability, which allows you to restrict your calendar search by name or type of event, or to notes.

Promote

This link provides HTML code and images for placing a button on your own Web site. When clicked, it will take users to the sign-up page for your group.

STARTING A YAHOO! GROUP

Are you convinced yet that Yahoo! Groups provide a very powerful means of communication and collaboration? You can start a group of your own in less than five minutes and discover that for yourself. It takes just three easy steps to get started, then another three to customize your group. Once it's up and running, the Management link on your group's page enables you to easily change settings and perform other group management tasks. Getting started involves entering information on three consecutive screens:

1. Select a Yahoo! Groups Category. Here you choose the appropriate Yahoo! directory category for your group. This page offers both a search box and the Groups directory to help you find the category in which your group best fits. Even if your group is private (not listed in the directory), you still must choose a category. Yahoo! staff members do browse through groups to make sure they are appropriately categorized. If they feel that yours is in the wrong category, they may move it to another. Consequently, it may take a few days for your group to appear in the directory.

2. Describe your Group. Enter a name for your group, an e-mail address for sending mail to the entire group, and a description of the group. When users search for groups to join, they're searching names and descriptions, so if you want them to find your group, be sure to include the obvious descriptive words. If your group's topic includes subtopics, you might want to mention those in the description. The description is limited to 200 characters.

3. Select your Yahoo! Profile and E-mail Address. The profile need not be the same one you use for other Yahoo! purposes. If you wish, you can create a profile specifically for this group—or you might elect to show no personal information at all, not even your real name. Your e-mail address is the one at which you want to receive messages from the group; it doesn't have to be a Yahoo! address.

After you've set up your group, Yahoo! presents you with several other options. You can come back later to complete these, if you prefer. The Customize option allows you to tailor the features you want to offer group members, and the degree of control that you, as owner, have over the group. You can specify whether the group is "public" and listed in the directory, whether members can join immediately or only with your approval, whether any member or only you, the owner, can post messages, whether messages require your (or a moderator's) approval before they're posted, whether replies go to all members or only to the person who posted the original message, and whether messages will be archived and, if so, who can view them. You also get to determine whether the group will have access to some or all of the additional Group features—files, calendar, polls, chat, photos, etc.—that I talked about earlier. For each of these features, you can specify who has access (members, nonmembers, moderators, owner only) and who can add, delete, or modify their content or configuration.

Inviting People To Join Your Group

If you're a moderator or owner of a group, your group pages include an "Invite" link. On the Invite Members page, you can add up to 50 members at a time by entering their e-mail addresses or Yahoo! IDs. A separate text box allows you to add an explanatory message to the e-mail invitation.

The e-mail that invitees receive includes a Join this Group link that takes them to a page with more information and an option to become a member of the group (and thereby take advantage of all its Web-based features) or just join the mailing list portion, which allows them to read and respond to group messages. If they opt to become a member, they then get to choose their profile and e-mail delivery options.

An alternative option, Add Members, allows you to automatically add up to 10 members per day, skipping the "invitation" and "acceptance" steps. The Invite Members page includes an Add Members link.

Managing Your Group

The Group Management Page makes it easy to review and modify the options available to a group. If you're the group owner, or a moderator with appropriate permission, you'll find a link to this page on your group's main page. The Management page is divided into the following sections.

Pending Tasks

If prospective members must be approved before they join the group, the Members link here lists any applicants that are awaiting approval. If the group is moderated and messages must be approved before posting, the Messages link indicates any messages awaiting approval.

Group Activity

This section includes links for Memberships, Message Posts, Web Features, E-mail Commands, and Moderator Activity. The owner and approved moderators can view all events related to group, specific member, and moderator activities. For instance, you can track invitations issued, members subscribed, messages posted, messages approved, files added, photos uploaded, and so on.

Group Settings

Group Settings allows owner/moderators to change such items as group description, membership type (open, restricted, by invitation), welcome message, and whether members' e-mail addresses display. They can also control access to group features such as chat, files, and photos, and determine who can post messages and how those messages appear.

Delete Group

With a click or two, the all-powerful owner can eliminate his or her group at will.

Yahoo! offers an alternative to changing group settings via the Group Management page. You can invoke a configuration "wizard" for a group you own or moderate by steering your browser to groups.Yahoo.com/group/*groupname*/confwiz (where *groupname* is the name of the group you want to reconfigure).

More About the Members Page

The Members page has been discussed from the perspective of the regular member. For owners and the moderators they've designated, the Members link on the group home page reveals some additional privileges. Owners and moderators see an "Edit" link beside each member's name. This enables them to change members' e-mail delivery preferences, remove members from the group, or ban them. Banning not only removes the member, but also prevents them from rejoining until the ban is lifted (Ah, the power!). At the other extreme, members can also be promoted to moderator or even to owner. Clicking the "Change to moderator" link opens the door to awarding a variety of privileges, including approving messages, approving prospective members, inviting members or banning them, changing moderator privileges, and others, including deleting the group.

ADDITIONAL POINTS ABOUT YAHOO! GROUPS

Anonymity and Privacy

We briefly discussed Yahoo! privacy considerations in Chapter 1. Keep in mind that Yahoo! itself has gathered some information from you, not only from what you input directly, but also from your ISP and your computer (see privacy.Yahoo.com/privacy). Yahoo! knows who you are. However, within Yahoo! Groups, you can maintain a relatively high level of anonymity from other users. Your profile need not contain any personal information. On the other hand, you may want to let others know who you are for a variety of reasons. The degree to which you "expose" yourself to other group users is largely up to you.

RSS Message Delivery

RSS (Really Simple Syndication), which is discussed in Chapters 3 and 5, is another way to keep up with your Yahoo! groups. Among the sources that Yahoo! offers in RSS are messages from groups to which you belong. A group owner must first have configured the group to make its messages "public." RSS enables you to receive new messages in your RSS reader, including, of course, the one you have set up on your My Yahoo! page. If you have a Weblog, you can send group messages there as well. To explore RSS delivery, click on the XML icon in the Recent Messages section of the Groups page, then follow the instructions.

Companion Toolbar

If you're using the Yahoo! Companion toolbar, you can add a Groups button. The arrow on that button displays a pull-down window with links for each group to which you belong. This is a very simple way to access your Groups main page in one click and any of your individual groups in just two.

YAHOO! GROUPS: AN INDISPENSABLE RESOURCE

Yahoo!'s enormous user population, its wide range of groups covering just about every subject you might imagine, its ease of use and accessibility to those who want to organize groups and those who simply want to use them, make it an indispensable resource for anyone who uses the Internet as a communications channel. Probably the best advice that can be offered regarding Yahoo! Groups is "Think of the possibilities!"

Yahoo! News

Whether you're a dedicated newshound, need to track a recent story on a particular topic, or just want to keep up on what's happening, Yahoo! News is a good place to start. Yahoo! has offered news since early in its history and now has one of the best news sites on the Web. Yahoo! News is not only fresh, extensive, and searchable, but beautifully integrated into other Yahoo! offerings such as My Yahoo! and Yahoo! Financial.

The strength of Yahoo! News is focused in three areas: the News home page with the day's headlines, the news search engine, and the news alert service. Each of these includes a variety of features, which we'll talk about in this chapter.

YAHOO!'S NEWS SOURCES

Yahoo! draws its news from more than 7,000 sources in 35 languages. This includes both news providers with which Yahoo! has licensing agreements and Web sources that it has identified and crawls on a constant basis. Yahoo! News sources include Reuters, the Associated Press (AP), Agence France-Presse (AFP), National Public Radio (NPR), *USA Today*, USNEWS.com, Canadian Press, Dow Jones, *Forbes*, *Financial Times*, *BusinessWeek Online*, *Investor's Business Daily*, and approximately 20 other providers. Also included are news sources from 45 U.S. cities. Different sources provide the content for various Yahoo! News categories. For example, Reuters, AP, and AFP provide the majority of main News page items, while E!Online only delivers content to the Entertainment category. News from the other 7,000 or so sources goes into the news database and is searchable, but does not appear on the News home page. The links to "Full Coverage" in the Yahoo! news pages refer to these 7,000 additional sources.

News from Reuters and the AP remains in Yahoo!'s News database for two weeks. News from other sources is typically retained for a month. This varies somewhat depending on the source; some stories may remain for as little as seven days. In general, don't expect to find news in Yahoo! that's older than a month. For a list of Yahoo! News sources, check help.yahoo.com/help/us/news/news-03.html.

YAHOO! NEWS HOME PAGE

Its "front page" presentation of headlines makes Yahoo! a popular choice for quickly checking on what's happening in the world (see Figure 5.1). Yahoo!'s News home page features a major headline in each of these categories: Top Stories, Business, World, Entertainment, Technology, Politics, Science, Health, Oddly Enough, and Op-Ed. Each category includes the headline, which is linked to the complete article, the source, how long ago the story appeared (in minutes and hours), and the lead paragraph. If the article includes a photo, you'll see a thumbnail image. Some stories include a link to video footage. A "Full Coverage" link leads to additional articles in that section. You can also look at all stories in a category by source (e.g., Reuters).

Yahoo!'s News Directory, which appears on the left side of the News home page, lets you quickly browse any of the topical news sections, as well as comics, weather, and audio and video clips. Click on any category to get headlines and links to subcategories. If you click on World, for example, the resulting page not only displays international news stories but a list of geographic subdivisions under World on the directory side of the page. Click on Europe, Middle East, or Canada to get news stories about those regions.

Figure 5.1 Yahoo! News Home Page (news.yahoo.com)

Beneath the News Directory are sections labeled Slideshows, Snapshots, Comics, Full Coverage, Resources, Services, News via RSS, and Audio/Video. Each of these provides more detailed access to Yahoo!'s news content and deserves a closer look:

- **Slideshows –** Click on Photo Highlight Slideshow for a display of featured photographs. The Gallery and Slideshow links lead to collections of photos on various themes, and photos on current news topics presented in slideshow format.

- **Snapshots –** The photos here are from a Yahoo! partner, such as USA Today, and link to additional images and features.

- **Comics –** Get your daily chuckle here from the day's featured cartoon, then click on More Comics for, you guessed it, more. There's a good chance you'll find your favorite comic strip here, since Yahoo! provides access to 40-plus well-known comics. Editorial cartoons get their own page, with current and recent contributions from 18 political cartoonists.

- **Full Coverage** – This section offers links to in-depth coverage of leading news stories, including relevant articles from all 7,000 sources that the Yahoo! search engine crawls. When you click on a story from one of the "crawled" sources, you go to that publication's own site rather than to a Yahoo! page. Regional, national, and international publications offer an additional wealth of stories, multimedia, archives, and other features, all presented with the style, perspective, and emphasis of that particular newspaper or other source.

- **Resources** – This miscellaneous collection includes News Web Sites (a link to the News and Media category of the Yahoo! Directory), News by Region (a link to the By Region subcategory of News and Media), What's New (in Yahoo!'s News offerings), News Message Boards (discussed later in this chapter), Corrections (aggregated corrections to stories from AP and Reuters), Today in History (from the AP feature by that name), Obituaries, and a site map for Yahoo! News.

- **Services** – From here you can set up and review your news and weather alerts. (See the section on Alerts later in this chapter.)

- **News via RSS** – This option lets you set up RSS feeds on your My Yahoo! page for various Yahoo! News categories and subcategories. RSS is discussed further later in this chapter.

- **Audio/Video** – This section features audio and video clips from selected sources, including Reuters, NPR, and AP. For a complete list of current clips, click Audio/Video in the News Directory further up the page.

News Story Pages

Click on a headline on the main News page to get the full text of any story (see Figure 5.2). As you read, you sometimes find a pair of "news - Web sites" links next to a term in the text, especially the name of a person, company, or organization. Click on "news" to run a news search on that term, and on "Web sites" to search Yahoo!'s Web database. Articles might include a photo, links to a slideshow of pictures, or a video related to the story.

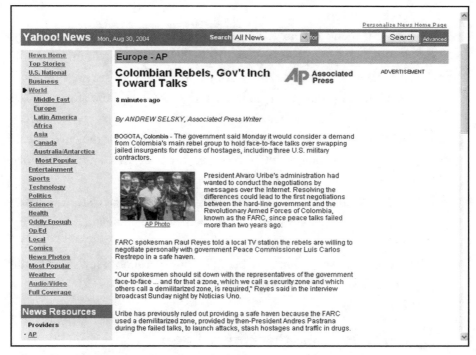

Figure 5.2 Yahoo! News Article Page

Take time to explore news story pages; you'll find a number of other useful features. The Yahoo! News Directory on the left side of the page shows the subdivisions of the category from which the current article came. For example, when you click on a headline from the Technology category, the subcategories for that category— Internet, Personal Technology, Communications, and several others—appear. You can browse the contents of these subcategories and make a mental note of areas that interest you. In the future you can go directly to these areas to keep up on the news you need to know. You also have the option, on this page, of adding that category to your My Yahoo! page (see Chapter 3).

If an article is about a publicly held company, a Related Quotes box appears on the page, showing stock prices (a few minutes delayed) for public companies mentioned in the story and for related companies as well. Click on a company's stock symbol to get more detailed information.

At the end of the article, Yahoo! may display links to related Web sites, as well as options for printing a "clean" copy, e-mailing the article to yourself or someone else, or discussing the topic in a Yahoo! group. Ratings links allow you to rate the story and see the average rating that others have assigned. A News Resources section links you to the Yahoo! News providers for the current category or subcategory. Click to see other stories in the category from that news provider.

News story pages also offer links to Full Coverage stories, which may include background and related news and features, opinions and editorials, and relevant Web sites. Clicking on articles in the Full Coverage section may take you out of Yahoo! News and to the site where the article originated.

Personalizing the News Page

The News home page features a "personalize" option that lets you specify the topical categories you want to see whenever you visit the page. In each category, you can choose to see either three or five headlines, with lead paragraphs if you want. You can also specify the order in which the categories appear on your page. For the weather section, you can select the cities worldwide for which you want to see weather conditions and forecasts. For that final decorator touch, you can also choose from one of seven color schemes. You must have a Yahoo! account and be signed in order to personalize the News page. Keep in mind that you can personalize your news even more extensively on your My Yahoo! page (see Chapter 4).

SEARCHING THE NEWS

You can search for stories on a specific topic from Yahoo!'s main page, Yahoo! Search (search.yahoo.com), the Yahoo! News home page (news.yahoo.com) or Advanced News Search page, or from the Yahoo! Companion toolbar. Whichever you use, you're covering not just the major Yahoo! News providers such as Reuters, NPR, and the AP, but also the 7,000 additional sites that Yahoo! crawls, including news sources from more than 35 countries.

You can also search the news using one of the "shortcuts" described in Chapter 2. Enter the word news followed by your term and you'll typically get a results page with three headlines on the topic, links to more headlines and "Full Coverage" of that topic, and links to the relevant categories in Yahoo!'s news directory.

When you search from the News home page, a pull-down window allows you to choose All News, Yahoo! News Only, News Photos, or Audio/Video. "All News" retrieves items from Yahoo! News providers and Yahoo!'s 7,000 crawled Web sites. "Yahoo! News Only" gets results from Reuters and Yahoo!'s other main news providers.

If you enter multiple terms in the search box, Yahoo! ANDs them together, meaning that the search engine will look for information in which *all* of your words occur. You can use an OR between terms to get stories in which either (or any) term appears. You can also use quotation marks to specify a phrase, and a minus sign in front of a term to exclude stories containing that term, for example mummy OR mummies egypt −movie. See Chapter 2 for more about searching with AND and OR.

Advanced News Search Page

The Advanced Search page offers many extra options and enables you to do more precise and flexible searching (see Figure 5.3). In addition to using Boolean by use of the menus you can search by headline, URL, date, source name, location, category, or language,

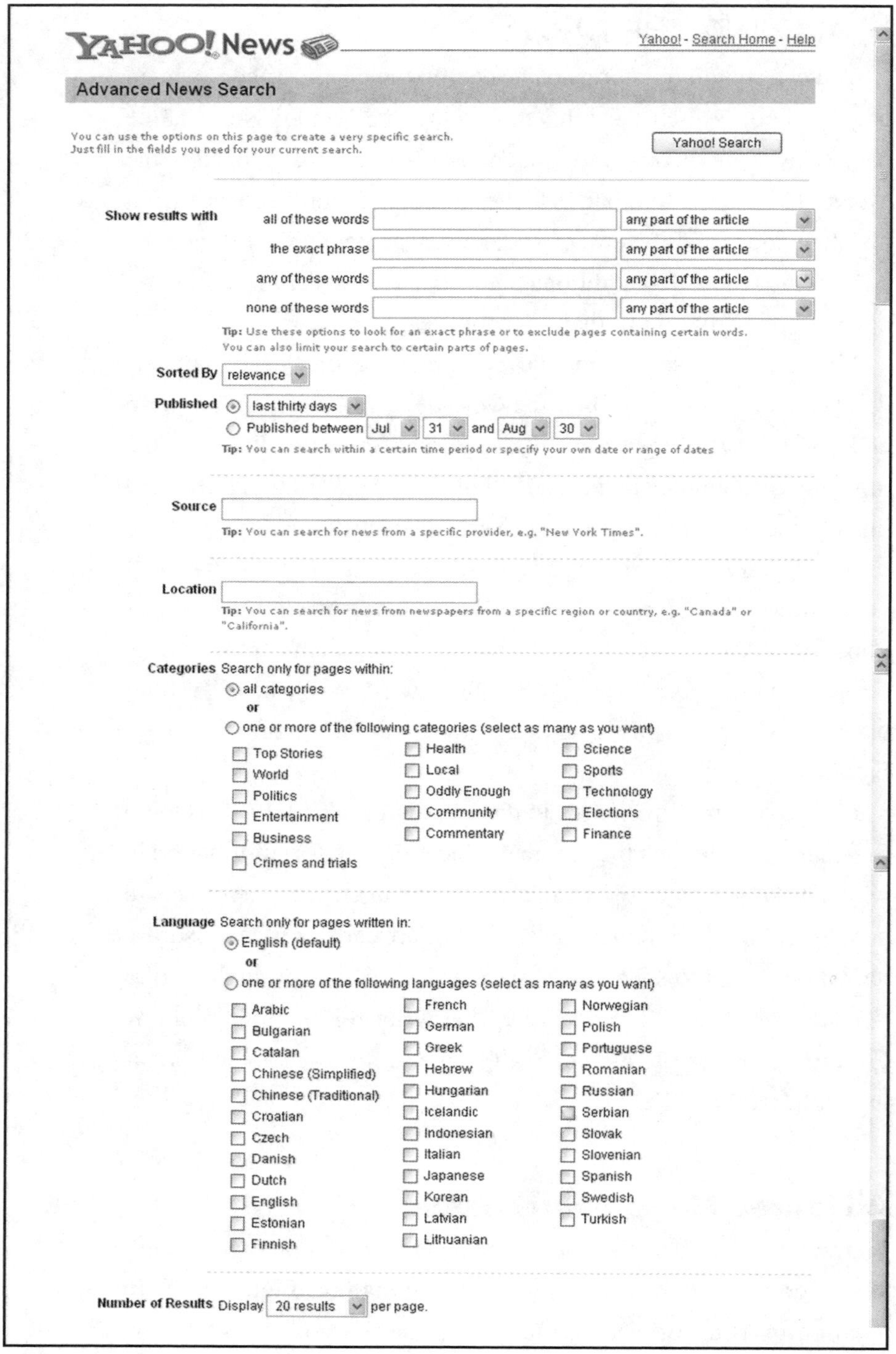

YAHOO! News

Yahoo! - Search Home - Help

Advanced News Search

You can use the options on this page to create a very specific search.
Just fill in the fields you need for your current search.

[Yahoo! Search]

Show results with

all of these words		any part of the article ▼
the exact phrase		any part of the article ▼
any of these words		any part of the article ▼
none of these words		any part of the article ▼

Tip: Use these options to look for an exact phrase or to exclude pages containing certain words.
You can also limit your search to certain parts of pages.

Sorted By [relevance ▼]

Published ◉ [last thirty days ▼]
○ Published between [Jul ▼] [31 ▼] and [Aug ▼] [30 ▼]

Tip: You can search within a certain time period or specify your own date or range of dates

Source [   ]

Tip: You can search for news from a specific provider, e.g. "New York Times".

Location [   ]

Tip: You can search for news from newspapers from a specific region or country, e.g. "Canada" or "California".

Categories Search only for pages within:

◉ all categories
or
○ one or more of the following categories (select as many as you want)

☐ Top Stories	☐ Health	☐ Science
☐ World	☐ Local	☐ Sports
☐ Politics	☐ Oddly Enough	☐ Technology
☐ Entertainment	☐ Community	☐ Elections
☐ Business	☐ Commentary	☐ Finance
☐ Crimes and trials		

Language Search only for pages written in:

◉ English (default)
or
○ one or more of the following languages (select as many as you want)

☐ Arabic	☐ French	☐ Norwegian
☐ Bulgarian	☐ German	☐ Polish
☐ Catalan	☐ Greek	☐ Portuguese
☐ Chinese (Simplified)	☐ Hebrew	☐ Romanian
☐ Chinese (Traditional)	☐ Hungarian	☐ Russian
☐ Croatian	☐ Icelandic	☐ Serbian
☐ Czech	☐ Indonesian	☐ Slovak
☐ Danish	☐ Italian	☐ Slovenian
☐ Dutch	☐ Japanese	☐ Spanish
☐ English	☐ Korean	☐ Swedish
☐ Estonian	☐ Latvian	☐ Turkish
☐ Finnish	☐ Lithuanian	

Number of Results Display [20 results ▼] per page.

Figure 5.3 Yahoo! Advanced News Search Page

and sort results by relevance or by date. You can also specify whether you want to see 10, 15, 20, 30, 40, or 100 items per results page. To get to the Advanced News Search page from Yahoo!'s home page, click News or In the News, then click Advanced Search. From the News home page (news.yahoo.com) or a news results page, just click on Advanced News Search.

Let's look at what you can do on the Advanced News Search page:

- **Show Results With –** Using the appropriate boxes at the top of the News search page, you can specify that "all of these words," "the exact phrase," "any of these words," or "none of these words" appear in your search results. If you do a search on the News home search page, you can click Advanced News Search on the first results page, and Yahoo! will transfer your query into the appropriate search boxes. You can then add some of the additional criteria that the Advanced News Search page offers. For instance, a pull-down window adjacent to those search boxes lets you limit your retrieval to any part of the article, the headline, or the URL.

- **Headlines and URL Searching –** Searching by headline gets you very precise results, but you may miss some highly relevant items that don't happen to have your search terms in the headline. Searching by URL lets you limit your search to a particular Web site, such as www.nytimes.com. In this case, you can only search by URL for "crawled" sources, since results from official Yahoo! News providers, such as Reuters or the *Chicago Tribune*, are delivered in the form of a Yahoo! page and have a Yahoo! URL. To limit to a particular news provider, try entering its name in the source box further down on the page. That will work whether you're looking for a Yahoo! News provider or a crawled source.

- **Sorted By –** By default, Yahoo! sorts search results by relevance. This window allows you to sort by date instead, an option that can be especially useful for very recent or rapidly breaking events.

- **Published** – The first radio button lets you narrow your results to items published in the last hour, day, week, two weeks, or 30 days. With the second radio button, you can be even more specific and limit to a given range of dates.

- **Source** – This is probably the best way to indicate that you only want articles from a particular news source. You can enter just a portion of the name, for example, "chicago," but if you're interested in the *Chicago Tribune*, put in the complete name, without quotation marks. Surprisingly, if you use quotation marks in this situation, you'll probably get results that are not from the news source you were after.

- **Location** – Specify a country, or a U.S. state or city, for news from—not about—that location.

- **Categories** – You can limit your search to one or more of Yahoo!'s 16 news categories, or let it default to "all."

- **Languages** – This option lets you restrict your search results to one or more of 35 listed languages, including English. For the main (U.S.) version of Yahoo!, the default is English.

- **Number of Results** – Here you can indicate how many items you want to see on each results page—10, 15, 20, 30, 40, or 100. More items per page take a little longer to load on a slow connection, but you can browse results more efficiently.

News Search Results Pages

For each matching record, Yahoo! shows the title of the article, linked to the full text, the source or publisher, a date and time stamp, and up to 40 words or so of the lead paragraph. However, the results pages consist of more than just a list of matching records (see Figure 5.4).

In the News Results section above your results listing, Yahoo! displays a recap of your search, with the total number of items found. Adjacent to that is a link to sort the results by date (latest first) instead of the default relevance ranking. Yahoo! offers "Also

Figure 5.4 News Search Results

try" suggestions for refining your results based on searches that others have done. For example, a search on "blackberry" might show:

Also try: rim blackberry, blackberry ban, blackberry patent

If you ran your search from the Advanced News Search page, the additional criteria you applied will appear under the search box. If, for example, you restricted your search to the World news category, to items from the last week, and to French-language items, you'd see the following line:

Show: *World* | from: *last week* | from: *all sources* | from: *all locations* | in *French*

Click on any of the specifications, such as *French*, and you'll go back to the place on the Advanced search page where you imposed that restriction. This feature makes it very easy to recall what you did in an Advanced search and to modify it if necessary. This line also appears at the bottom of results pages.

Near the search box you'll also find the standard Yahoo! options for running your search in the Web, Images, Directory, Yellow Pages, or Products databases. The search box and alternate database links also appear at the bottom of the page. Note that Directory refers to Yahoo!'s general Web directory, not the News directory; the same is true of the Images option. See Chapter 2 for more about Yahoo!'s searchable databases.

However, Yahoo! automatically includes news photos and other multimedia when you run a news search. Depending on your search, the right side of the page may display up to three related photos from a Yahoo! news provider such as Reuters, AP, or AFP. Click on any image for a larger version and perhaps a slideshow of related images. A "More Image results for..." link leads to other news images that match your search. If you're primarily searching for images, you'll like this news images results page, which provides a description of each image and links to related news articles. Links to any audio/video results appear below the "More Image..." link. The speaker and TV symbols indicate an audio or a video clip, respectively.

Searching for News Images

As mentioned, Yahoo! retrieves related images automatically when you do a news search and displays up to three on your results page. Alternatively, you can look for photos starting on the Yahoo! News home page, by clicking on the News Photo link in the News Directory and then browsing through subcategories.

You can also search directly for news images without doing a subject search first. On the Yahoo! News home page, select News Photos in the window next to the search box, then enter your search terms. The image search results page displays images with brief descriptions, plus links to news stories, and audio and video clips. Click on a photo to see a larger version. The resulting page also has options for e-mailing, printing, and rating the image.

If you're searching for images, don't overlook the Slideshow links that appear throughout Yahoo! News. You can browse by broad category, such as Top Stories, World, Sports, Entertainment, Lifestyle, Science, Politics, Business, or Technology, or select from the currently most popular slideshows. You can move easily from photo to photo in the slideshow you choose by clicking on Start, Next, and Previous. The "multi-photos" option allows you to view several images at once. This can be very helpful, especially if you're looking for a particular picture, since some slideshows consist of more than 200 images.

Searching for News Audio and Video

Like news photos, audio and video results are integrated into your basic Yahoo! news searches. You can also get to these multimedia resources by clicking on the Audio/Video link in the directory section of the News home page, or by searching from the News home page and selecting Audio/Video from the pull-down window. Yahoo! News' audio and video content remains available for about two weeks, and is supplied by AP, Reuters, NPR, and washingtonpost. com. (Remember that the Full Coverage sources provide access to a lot more multimedia.)

If you want to browse through the Yahoo! News audio and video collection, click Audio/Video on the News home page to get to the main audio/video page. From there you can browse by topic category or provider. Items are listed in date order, most recent first. At the bottom of these pages is a window that allows you to search audio/video by a specific date.

IMPORTANT YAHOO! NEWS FEATURES

News Alerts

News alerts notify you automatically when new information is published on a topic of your choice. You can get your alerts via e-mail, Yahoo! Messenger, or your mobile device. News alerts in general are one of the most undervalued and underused offerings on the Internet. Just a very few years ago, many corporations and other organizations paid tens of thousands of dollars per year for the kind of alerting services that Yahoo! and others now provide for free. Every serious Yahoo! user should give Yahoo!'s alerts a try. (This doesn't necessarily mean that you should cancel news alerts you might be running, for a fee, on commercial online services. Those services might provide access to sources that Yahoo! doesn't cover.)

You must have a Yahoo! account in order to use alerts. (If you don't have a Yahoo! account by now, I have failed.) If you do not yet have an account, you'll be led through the sign-up process as you begin to set up an alert.

To create an alert, use the News Alerts link under Services on the News home page, or on any news search results page. The first is more powerful because it gives you more options; the latter is easier because it involves fewer steps. Yahoo! allows a maximum of 30 alerts per account. This limit covers all types of Yahoo! Alerts, including News, Auction, Weather, and Stock. All News Alerts provide an e-mail delivery option, among others. You can specify any account you want for e-mail delivery; it doesn't have to be a Yahoo! e-mail address. E-mail alerts include a link in each message that allows you to cancel the alert.

Clicking the News Alerts link on the News home page brings up your own Alerts page. Here you can set up three kinds of alerts: Keyword News, Daily News Digest, and Breaking News. Your Alerts page lists any alerts you currently have running, and lets you modify or delete your alerts.

Keyword News alerts deliver results based on an ongoing search for one or more terms you specify (see Figure 5.5). When setting up a keyword alert, enter your search terms in the "Include" box, enter any "NOT" words in the "Do not include" box, and specify the delivery method (e-mail, Yahoo! Messenger, or mobile device). Under e-mail, click Change Delivery Options if you prefer plain text formatting rather than HTML, or if you'd rather get immediate delivery of individual items as Yahoo! receives them, as opposed to the default "Once Daily." If you select mobile delivery, you specify the device type and your daily message limit, as well as registering the device itself with Yahoo!.

Be a bit careful when creating your alert, since terms are automatically ANDed. If you want an alert on either Munich or München, you'll need to set up two alerts. (Actually, you'll have to set up the second one as "Muenchen," since that's how Yahoo! deals with umlauts.) You can use quotation marks to indicate a phrase search.

Every time you do a News search, you'll see a News Alert button for setting up a keyword alert on the topic.

Daily News Digests deliver news from the Yahoo! News categories of your choice, including Front Page, Top Stories, and Most Popular, as well as topical categories such as Business and Technology. To set up a Daily News Digest, you simply select your category or categories, and specify delivery via e-mail or mobile device. Again, you'll have to supply Yahoo! with information about the latter, if you haven't done so previously. You can opt to receive

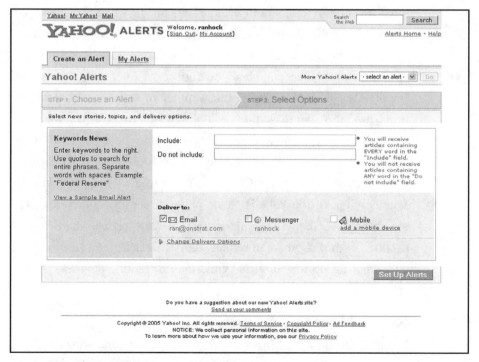

Figure 5.5 Setting Up a Keyword Alert

e-mail in plain text or HTML format, and specify the time of day you want to receive it.

Breaking News is the broadest of the alert options. To set up a Breaking News Alert, you choose either AP or Reuters and the delivery method—e-mail, mobile device, or Yahoo! Messenger. Delivery is immediate, as stories break. See Table 5.1 for a comparison of news alerts.

Yahoo! Weather

Yahoo! Weather is discussed in some detail in Chapter 9, Other Seriously Useful Yahoo! Stuff, but needs to be mentioned here as well because it's so highly integrated with Yahoo! News. The first time you visit the Weather section of the Yahoo! News home page, you'll see a Select Your City link that allows you to customize your weather reports and forecasts. For U.S. cities, the choices can be *very* local. In Maryland, for example, you can choose from more than 400 cities, towns, and villages. In the rest of the world, you might not be able to get as focused, but most countries offer dozens, sometimes hundreds, of weather locations from which to choose.

The Yahoo! News page lets you choose weather for just one city. If you want a quick view of the weather in several selected locations, use the Weather section of your My Yahoo! page. But the main Yahoo! Weather page (weather.yahoo.com) is where you can satisfy all of your weather needs and urges. The information on this page is provided by the Weather Channel. You can also get there via the Weather link in the Yahoo! News page Directory. The News page also offers Weather Alerts, along with News Alerts, in the Services section. With this, you can request daily forecasts, at a time of your choosing, for up to four cities via e-mail or mobile device.

News Message Boards

The Yahoo! News Message Boards enable anyone with a Yahoo! account to comment on specific news articles from Yahoo!'s News

Table 5.1 Comparing Yahoo! Alert Options

	You select:	Coverage	Delivery Method	Frequency
Keyword News	Keywords	Yahoo! News providers	E-mail, mobile device, or Yahoo! Messenger	Once per day or immediately
Daily News Digest	News categories	Yahoo! News providers	E-mail or mobile service	Once per day
Breaking News	AP or Reuters	AP or Reuters	E-mail, mobile device, or Yahoo! Messenger	Immediately

providers. You can get to the discussions by clicking on the News Message Boards link in the Resources section of the Yahoo! News pages, or on the Post/Read Messages link below a Yahoo! News story.

Clicking on the former will take you to the main Yahoo! News Message Boards page. To find the discussion of a particular story, browse the directory of message board discussions and click on the story you want to discuss. The Search box on the Yahoo! News Message Boards page leads you directly to individual stories, from which you can get to discussions via the Post/Read messages link.

The message board for a particular story displays a list of the messages that have been posted. Click on a message title to get the complete text. You can navigate the News message boards quite easily using the navigation links—Previous, Next, First, Last, Post New Message, etc. If you use message boards frequently, you may grow to appreciate, even love, the "Ignore this User" option.

Yahoo! News Message Boards are just one component of the Yahoo! Message Boards collection. For a more detailed discussion of Yahoo!'s Message Boards, see Chapter 6, Yahoo!: The Great Communicator.

News Via My Yahoo!

There are many ways to get to the news through Yahoo! and many ways for that news to get to you. The Yahoo! News page is an obvious starting place, and Yahoo! Alerts are a good way to monitor the news that matters to you. My Yahoo!, to which Chapter 3 is devoted, is another excellent way to keep up with the news. With My Yahoo!, you can view headlines from news sources that you have chosen whenever you go to My Yahoo!. Click on the Add Content link on your My Yahoo! page and then choose from 200,000 sources (most of that number comprised of Weblogs and other RSS feeds) and place those modules on your My Yahoo! page; stories from the sources you choose are then automatically fed to you so you can see headlines or summaries, and then go from there directly to the source. See Chapter 3 for more details. If you have made My Yahoo! the home or "start" page for your browser, you'll see current headlines, tailored to your interests, every time you go online.

Yahoo! RSS Feeds

Depending on whom you ask, RSS stands for "Really Simple Syndication" or "Rich Site Summary," or both. Whichever meaning is the "true" one, they mean essentially the same thing. RSS is a format by which news providers, however loosely you define that term, can easily syndicate, or distribute, their content. RSS utilizes XML, which is a cousin (on its mother's side) of HTML, the language in which most Web sites are written. Using RSS, Yahoo! gathers headlines from a broad range of sources and creates links to the stories. Yahoo! uses RSS to syndicate its own content to others, and also takes advantage of the same technology to gather headlines from news publishers and make them available within My Yahoo!. RSS extends the range of My Yahoo! news sources tremendously. An ever-increasing number of the 7,000 sites that Yahoo! now crawls provide their content through RSS. Yahoo! has been aggressively pursuing those news providers in order to pass those news feeds on to you.

It is easy to take advantage of RSS by using My Yahoo! As a matter of fact, you may take good advantage of it without even noticing that the news you are getting is provided by means of RSS. With My Yahoo!, 200,000 RSS feeds are available for you to choose from. Up to 100 of them can be placed as modules on a My Yahoo! page. For details, see Chapter 3.

In addition to using My Yahoo! to locate RSS sources of interest, you may have noticed that some stories you find in various places on the Web, even outside of Yahoo!, have an "Add to My Yahoo!" button next to them. When you find such a story you can just click the button and the source will be added to your My Yahoo! page.

If you run across a site that indicates it has an RSS feed, by a little orange "XML" or "RSS" button, but does not have the Add to My Yahoo! button, you can still add it to your My Yahoo! page. Click on the XML button on the site you found. Ignore the page of code that comes up, but go up to your browser's address bar and copy the URL. The go to My Yahoo! and click on the Add Content button. To the right of the Search box (in the "Find" section of the Add Content page) you will see a link for "Add RSS by URL." Click on that and copy the URL you found into the URL entry box on that page. Yahoo! will ask if you really want to add it. Say yes by clicking the Add button. When you go to My Yahoo!, you will have that source on your page.

News on the Companion Toolbar

Wait! Here's one more way of easily getting to Yahoo! News sources. If you've installed the Yahoo! Companion Tool Bar (discussed in Chapter 1), you may already have a News button. If not, you can click on the Toolbar Setting icon (the pencil), then on Add/Edit Buttons, and finally choose the News button. With that button on the Toolbar, you can either click and go directly to the Yahoo! News home page, or click on the arrow next to the button and choose one of the Top Stories or news categories in the pull-down window. Regardless of where you are on the Web, the News button on the Yahoo! Companion Toolbar puts you just a click or two away from what's happening in the world.

International Coverage

At the beginning of this chapter it was mentioned that Yahoo! News comes in 35 different languages. This in itself indicates that

Yahoo!'s News is much more international in scope than many news sites. In the "Searching the News" section of this chapter you saw that you can use the Advanced News Search page to limit your retrieval to any of those languages. Yahoo! offers one more approach to non-English and/or non-U.S. materials—its 22 country-specific "local" versions. Most country versions of Yahoo! have a News home page equivalent to the main Yahoo! News page we've been discussing here. The stories in those local versions are usually more relevant to the particular region than those on the main Yahoo!.

THE BEST PLACE FOR NEWS

Yahoo! delivers news through many channels—My Yahoo!, Yahoo! Financial, Yahoo! Sports, and others. This chapter focuses primarily on the biggest, most searchable, and most concentrated collection of news content and resources, the Yahoo! News home page. Depending on your news needs, this may be the place to start. Or perhaps you'll find other routes, such as My Yahoo! and the Yahoo! Companion Toolbar, more convenient for your purposes. You may find that specialized locations, such as Yahoo! Financial, are best for the news you need. Use what works for you, but remain aware of the richness of Yahoo!'s news offerings and the variety of ways you can get to them.

CHAPTER 6

Yahoo!, The Great Communicator

Like the Internet itself, Yahoo! is, in a sense, all about communication. Parts of Yahoo!, though, focus directly on people communicating with people, not just Web pages communicating to an audience. This is especially true of Yahoo! Mail, Messenger, Message Boards, Chat, Geocities, and Yahoo! Groups. Chapter 4 is completely devoted to Yahoo! Groups and everything you can do there. Now it's time to deal with Yahoo!'s other communication venues. We'll look at each of them in turn.

YAHOO! MAIL

There are several reasons to use Yahoo! Mail, even if you have other e-mail accounts. It's always wise to have a backup or secondary e-mail account, just in case, and Yahoo! Mail is a good choice. It provides all the basic features you expect in an e-mail system. Not only that, it's integrated into other Yahoo! functions in ways that enhance both those functions and Yahoo! Mail itself.

In addition to sending and receiving messages and attachments, Yahoo! Mail provides an address book, facilities for storing, sorting, and searching your e-mail, access to your other (POP) e-mail accounts, spam filtering, virus protection, automated "on vacation" responses, and a number of options for displaying and handling your outgoing and incoming messages. Yahoo!'s Premium service, Mail Plus, offers a few additional features.

Signing Up

You can sign up for a Yahoo! e-mail account by clicking Mail at the top of the main Yahoo! page and following the instructions. Alternatively, when you sign up for My Yahoo!, simply check the box for activating your Yahoo! Mail account. In either case, you then specify your Yahoo! ID and password, establish a security question and answer, supply your full name, gender, ZIP or Postal code, industry, title, and specialization, and indicate whether you want your name and address listed in Yahoo! People Finder. The Yahoo! Terms of Service require that you "provide true, accurate, current and complete information about yourself." You can also opt to receive offers and surveys in selected categories.

A word about choosing your Yahoo! ID: Keep in mind that millions of Yahoo! users have preceded you, and the simplest IDs, like "Rosebud," are long gone. Try, though, to select an ID that will be at least vaguely recognizable by people you know, so they won't automatically delete a message from you as spam. Some combination of your first and last name or initials might suffice, or your name plus ZIP code or year of birth, or even "Rosebud" followed by a number that nobody else has gotten to first.

The Main Yahoo! Mail Page

Familiarize yourself with the main Mail features by poking around on the main Mail page (see Figure 6.1). You'll find features such as:

- **Tabs for Yahoo! Address Book, Calendar, and Notepad,** with quick access to their main features
- **Check Mail button** – to access your inbox and messages
- **Compose button** – to create new e-mail messages.
- **Search Mail button** – to search for messages by sender, subject, specific term, etc.

- **Mail Upgrades link –** to upgrade, for a fee, to Yahoo!'s premium service
- **Mail Options link –** to change message display or spam settings, block unwanted senders, filter mail into various folders, add a signature to your messages, customize your inbox view, send automated responses, etc.
- **Check Other Mail section –** to check one or more of your non-Yahoo! e-mail accounts for new messages. This section will not appear until you have set up a connection to your other e-mail accounts by using the "Mail Accounts" section of Mail Options.
- **Folders section –** to access and manage the folders in which your messages are stored
- **Folder/Message display window –** the largest portion of the main Mail page is the area in which folder contents and messages are displayed. When you first log on, this section

Figure 6.1 Yahoo! Mail Main Page

contains a welcome message and a bar showing how much of your 250 MB of free storage space you're currently using. The welcome screen also displays how many unread messages you have, and in which folders.

Sending Messages

Click the "Compose" button to start writing an e-mail message. You'll get a familiar-looking screen with a To: box for recipients (be sure to separate multiple e-mail addresses with a comma) and Cc: and Bcc: links to add boxes for copies and blind copies (see Figure 6.2). If you've assigned nicknames to contacts in your Address Book, you can use the nicknames instead of e-mail addresses. You can send messages to as many as 100 recipients at a time, including those you cc: or bcc: A single message is limited to 10 MB.

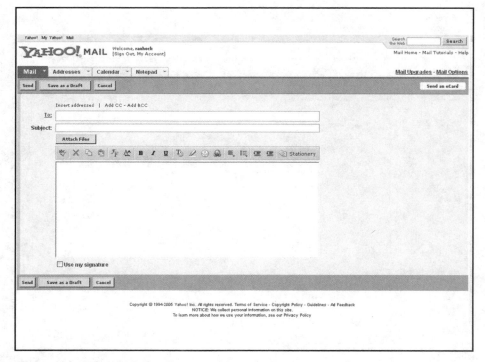

Figure 6.2 Yahoo! Mail – Compose Message Screen

The main part of the compose screen is the window in which you type or paste your message. Text can be "processed" using the buttons above the message window. Your options are: spell check, cut, copy, paste, font face, font size, bold, italic, underline, text color, highlight color, insert emoticon, insert hyperlink, align text, bullet list, decrease indent, and increase indent. (If these options do not appear, go to the Mail Options page and under General Preferences - Composing E-mails, choose the color and graphics option. This option will probably work only in Internet Explorer 5.5 or higher.) Mail Plus subscribers can add a "stationery" background to their messages is. The emoticon button gives you 40 "smileys" from which to choose.

Click Attach Files to send e-mail attachments. You can add up to five files at a time. Click Attach More Files if you want to send more than five in a single message. After selecting your files, click Attach and then Done. Your Compose window returns, showing the list of files that you've attached.

Buttons at both the top and the bottom of the page allow you to send your message at this point, save it as a draft, or cancel the operation. Save as Draft stores the unsent message in your Drafts folder. You also have the option of saving a copy of the message in your Sent folder and of adding your "signature" file (you must activate these options first under Mail Options).

Viewing Received Messages

To read your e-mail, click the Check Mail button or the Inbox link in the Folders section. For each message, you'll see the sender, subject, date, and size of message. To read a message, click on the subject. By default, messages display by date, most recent first. Click on the Sender, Subject, or Size header to sort by any of those criteria.

In front of a Sender you may see an address book contact card icon if the sender is in your Yahoo! Address Book, a left arrow for messages you've replied to, and a right arrow for messages you've forwarded. A paper clip icon preceding the subject header indicates that the message has an attachment.

To the left of each message line is a checkbox, which you can use to select one or more messages before using the "Delete," "Spam," Mark," or "Move" buttons. "Delete" sends the message to the Trash folder. "Spam" not only deletes it but also reports it to Yahoo! as spam. If you mark a message as spam, a page comes on which you can elect to block any further messages from that sender. The Mark button enables you to mark selected records as Unread or Read, or to flag (and unflag) them for follow-up. The Move button lets you transfer checked messages to another folder.

A View link at the top of the message list lets you change the default from View - All Messages to one of the following:

- **Messages from My Contacts –** This will display only messages from people in your Yahoo! Address Book.

- **Messages from Unknown Senders –** These are messages from people who are not in your address book.

- **Unread Messages –** Yes, these are messages you haven't read.

- **Flagged Messages –** These messages you have flagged for follow-up or other reasons.

Use the First, Previous, Next, and Last links at the bottom and top of the list to navigate among your messages. The appearance and functionality of your other e-mail folders is similar to that of the Inbox.

Viewing a Specific Message

Click on the subject of any message in your Inbox or other mail folder to view the actual message. You can delete, reply to, or forward the message, as well as move it to another folder or mark it as spam. You can generate a "printable view," look at full headers (which include lots of technical information about the originating IP and the route your message took on its way to you), flag or unflag the message, or add the sender to your Yahoo! Address Book.

If the message includes attachments, you'll see a paper clip icon and, at the end of the message, information about each attachment, along with a Scan and Download Attachment link. "Scan" means that Yahoo! will scan the file for viruses and, assuming it's "clean," offer a link to download it to your computer. If the attachment is an image, you get a second option—Scan and Save to my Yahoo! Photos. For Microsoft Word or Excel files, your additional options are Scan and Save to My Briefcase (see Chapter 3 for details on My Briefcase) or View Attachment. For HTML attachments the file will show up in the window as a Web page and provide a link to download. What you see when dealing with attachments may vary depending on the type of file, and on how the message was handled by the e-mail program on the sending end.

Folders

The Folders section on the left of your Yahoo! Mail page lists the standard folders—Inbox, Draft, Sent, Bulk, Trash—and, under those, any folders you have created yourself (see Figure 6.1). Beside each folder, in parentheses, is the number of unread messages it contains. Click on any folder name to see its contents. The Bulk folder contains messages that Yahoo! suspects are spam and sent to this folder automatically, rather than to your Inbox. Since spam-filtering is an inexact science, it's a good idea to check this folder periodically to make sure mail you want hasn't inadvertently been tagged as spam. You can identify a message in the Bulk folder as "not spam" to have it automatically moved to your Inbox. Yahoo! deletes the contents of your Bulk mail box after a month, unless you have specified a shorter period (more about this in the Mail Options section that follows). Items in your Bulk and Trash folders don't count against your storage limit, but you should get in the habit of emptying both on a regular basis.

The Add button allows you to quickly create a new folder. The Edit button takes you to a list of your folders with information about the number of messages in each, the number of unread messages, and the total size of the contents. Folders you created include links for renaming or deleting them. You can also create new folders on this page.

Search Mail

Most Yahoo! Mail pages include a Search Mail option that lets you look for messages containing particular words. If you enter multiple words, they will be ANDed together, which means you'll get only those messages that contain all the words you entered. A checkbox on the search page allows you to make your search case-sensitive. You can also opt to search All Folders or just the one you specify.

The Search options let you search the From and To lines, including Cc: and Bcc:, the subject header, and the body of the message, individually or in combination. You can specify that any or all of these "contains," "does not contain," "begins with," or "is exactly" the term or name you're searching for. The Advanced Search page also enables you to narrow results to messages sent on a specific date or dated before or after a specific date. You can search all messages, or limit your search to messages you've read or not read, or to a particular folder or folders.

Mail Options

The Mail Options link enables you to tailor several aspects of your Yahoo! Mail.

Spam Protections

Yahoo! Mail's SpamGuard program addresses the spam problem in several ways. It automatically identifies messages that it suspects are spam, and sends them to your Bulk mail folder. It also allows *you* to identify messages as spam, block the sender so you don't receive e-mail from them in the future, and report the sender to Yahoo!. The Options page lets you turn the spam filter off and on, immediately delete messages that SpamGuard identifies as suspect, or keep such messages in the Bulk folder for one or two weeks instead of a month. Some spam messages contain images and graphics that, when you open the message, automatically verifies the validity of your e-mail address to the spammer. SpamGuard automatically blocks images that it suspects of doing this. On the Options page, you can specify that Yahoo! Mail block no images or *all* images. The Anti-Spam Resource Center portion of the page provides detailed information about SpamGuard and background information on industry efforts to combat spam.

Blocking Addresses

This section of the Options page lets you enter up to 100 e-mail addresses of senders whose messages you want blocked. It also allows you to remove senders from your blocked list.

Filters

Filters allow you to automatically direct certain messages to a folder other than your inbox. This can be incredibly useful if you get large quantities of e-mail and want to prioritize your reading, or simply want to manage your mail more effectively. Click on Filters, then on the Add button. Give the filter a name, then configure it by identifying which part of the message to look at (Header, To/Cc, Subject, or Body), the word or name to look for, whether to match case, and the condition to apply: "contains," "does not contain," "begins with," or "ends with" the term you entered. You then indicate the destination folder for those filtered messages. You can also create a new folder at this point. Return to the Filters page if you need to edit or delete filters you've created. Regular Yahoo! Mail lets you set up as many as 15 filters. MailPlus gives you up to 100.

Management > Mail Accounts

This section allows you to modify the appearance and handling of your Yahoo! Mail as well as other e-mail accounts that you may want to access through Yahoo! Mail. From the first Mail Accounts screen, choose the account you wish to change and then click the Edit button. For Yahoo! Mail, you can change your "From" name and "Reply to" address, the date order in which messages display, the number of messages per page, whether copies of sent messages go to your Sent folder and unsolicited mail goes to the Bulk folder, whether to show full versus brief headers, whether to block HTML graphics, whether to display warning messages under various conditions, where the program takes you after moving or deleting a message, whether forwarded messages are sent as inline text or attachments, how much of the original message to include when replying, and whether AutoComplete is on or off. You can change your font size and screen width in this section.

You can also set up Yahoo! to check your other e-mail accounts for new messages. This can be particularly useful if you're traveling and can't get to those accounts via the Web. To add a new account, click Add, then provide a name for it (e.g., "work"), the address of the POP (Post Office Protocol) mail server (e.g., mail.lesley.edu), your user name and password for that account, and a color indicator that will appear next to "outside" messages to distinguish them from your Yahoo! Mail messages. You can use the Edit button to change any of this information, and to specify whether mail should be left on the server (a good idea if you want to retrieve it again when you get home or back to the office), whether to retrieve new messages only, and whether to filter these messages.

Personalization > General Preferences

Personalization > General Preferences options are identical to the ones described earlier for your Yahoo! Mail account.

Personalization > Signature

In this section, you can set up an e-mail "signature" to append to your e-mail messages. You can select plain or formatted text, include HTML (such as a link to your business or personal home page), and add an emoticon (smiley) if you must. You can specify that the signature be attached to all messages, or leave that option unchecked and decide whether to include the signature with certain messages only. Note that the free version of Yahoo! Mail includes a permanent, nonremoveable footer at the bottom of every message you send. This says something like "DO YOU YAHOO!? Get your free @yahoo.com address at http://mail. yahoo.com."

Personalization > Vacation Response

Here you can compose a brief message that Yahoo! will send out automatically to anyone who e-mails you during the "vacation" period you choose. You might want to say something like "I'm away from my computer until the week of the 15th but if your message requires a response, I'll get back to you then." You can also create a separate message that will go out in response to any messages from one or two selected domains.

Premium Services > Mail Plus

Among other features, Mail Plus offers additional spam and virus protection, gets rid of graphical ads in your mail, provides added storage (up to two GB), and allows you to use other mail programs, such as Outlook, to read your Yahoo! Mail. Of course, you pay a fee for all these extras.

Premium Services > Personal Address

The Personal Address premium service provides up to five addresses with your own domain name in the address instead of @yahoo.com.

Premium Services > Business Mail

The Business Mail option offers 10 e-mail accounts at your own domain name, more storage, and several other features.

Your Yahoo! Address Book

The Yahoo! Address Book has numerous applications in addition to its use with Yahoo! Mail. Some of these applications are discussed elsewhere in this book, particularly in Chapter 3. In conjunction with Mail, the Address Book provides a quick and easy way to store and use e-mail addresses (see Figure 6.3).

When you receive a message, you can add the sender to your Address Book by clicking "Add to Address Book" on the From: line of the message. At the same time, you can add a nickname and a phone number if you have it.

If you have AutoComplete turned on when you're composing a message, Yahoo! will check your Address Book and identify possible matches as you start typing the e-mail address. You can select from the list of names rather than typing (and trying to remember!) the whole address. The Address Book also lets you create lists of e-mail addresses that eliminate the need to enter each address individually when sending e-mail to multiple recipients. Consider using this feature if you routinely e-mail members of a club, committee, or other group of people. To use one of your lists, click on To:, Cc:, or Bcc: on the Compose screen. Select the list and/or individuals you want from the pop-up Address Book window.

You must create your lists in the Address Book, rather than from within Mail, but the Address Book is readily available via the tab that appears on most Mail screens. Click the down arrow on that tab for immediate access to Add List and other Address Book functions.

Optimizing Your Storage Capacity

Yahoo! provides you with 250 megabytes of free e-mail storage. That's quite a bit, enough for tens of thousands of average messages.

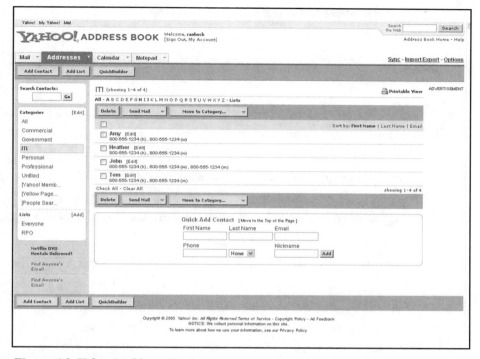

Figure 6.3 Yahoo! Address Book

What *does* take up space, though, are attachments. To make the best use of your storage allotment, check your Mail folders periodically for messages with large attachments. Download any you want to save to your own computer, then delete the messages from Yahoo! Mail. Don't overlook your Sent folder. If you forwarded a message with a large attachment, that attachment is still taking up space in your Sent folder. Also keep in mind that you can upgrade to Mail Plus, for a fee, and get 2 gigabytes of storage. Now, that's a *lot*.

Streamlining Access to Yahoo! Mail

There are lots of ways to get to your Yahoo! Mail page. Making it a module on your My Yahoo! page (see Chapter 3) gives you immediate access to Mail as well as many other Yahoo! features. If you install a Mail button on your Yahoo! Companion Toolbar, one click takes you to the main Yahoo! Mail page. Even better, the down arrow on the Mail button lets you access basic mail functions right from the toolbar.

YAHOO! MESSENGER

Instant messaging (IM) is a lot like e-mail, and even easier in some ways. With IM, you exchange messages in real time with other people who are online at the same time you are. Unlike e-mail, where you may not get a reply any time soon, with IM you usually hear back almost immediately. IM typically is conducted in a small window on your screen that you can access while working with other programs (see Figure 6.4). With Yahoo! Messenger, Yahoo!'s instant messaging service, you can send and receive not only plain text messages, but fancier, formatted text, as well as photos and other files. You can also communicate via audio messages, use your Webcam for a video conversation, talk with multiple people in conferencing mode, send text messages to a cell phone, play games such as chess with another online participant, and listen to radio stations using Messenger. Yahoo! Messenger is integrated very well with other Yahoo! services; you can receive Yahoo! News and e-mail alerts via Messenger, and even conduct a Yahoo! Web search jointly with another person.

There are, however, a few barriers to sending your first IM. First, you must download the Messenger program; that's easy and quick. The big issue is that Yahoo! has several competitors in the IM arena, including AOL and MSN; unfortunately, these various systems don't talk to each other (yet). If you use Yahoo! Messenger exclusively and your friend just uses AOL's service, you won't be able to send messages to each other. Consequently, you must convince your friends to download and use Yahoo! Messenger. (They'll do it if they really love you. Or if you're their boss. Or maybe with only a minimal amount of encouragement on your part.) By the way, "friend" is one of the standard terms used to refer to people with whom you

IM. You may not even like them. In some IM systems, they're referred to as Buddies.

The Messenger program takes just a few minutes to download and install if you have a high-speed connection. There are Windows, Mac, and UNIX versions. To download Messenger, go to Yahoo!'s main page and click on the Messenger link. Then click on "Get It Now" and follow the instructions.

Signing On

Once you've downloaded Messenger, click on the program's icon on your desktop. Then enter your regular Yahoo! ID and password in the Sign-In window. The three checkboxes on the sign-in window deserve attention: If you check "Remember my ID and password," they will appear automatically in the sign-in window the next time you load Messenger. All you need to do then is click "Sign in." If you check "Automatically sign in," you don't even have to do that.

Figure 6.4 Yahoo! Messenger Windows (Main Messenger and IM)

Of course, selecting either of these means that if someone else uses your computer, they can say all kinds of interesting things to your friends under your name. The third option, "Sign in as invisible" allows you to be signed in without other people knowing it. Friends who have your name on their Messenger List (which I'll talk about shortly) will see an indication that you are "offline."

Once you start using Messenger, you'll work primarily in two kinds of windows, the main Messenger window and individual IM windows. The main Messenger window gives you access to Messenger in general, with all of its functions, and the IM windows control your interaction with a specific contact or contacts. You can have many IM windows open at the same time.

In the following sections, we'll look at how you add contacts and then send and receive messages with those contacts. After that, we'll examine a variety of useful, powerful, and just plain cool features built into Messenger. Finally, we'll come back to familiarize our-selves—that is, *you*—with the rest of the main Messenger window.

Adding Contacts

Before you send a message to someone, they must be on your Messenger List. You'll need that person's Yahoo! ID or their e-mail address. Click the Add icon on the Messenger window. Then, on the Add to Messenger List screen, enter their Yahoo! ID or e-mail address, and choose a name by which to identify them. You also need to indicate the "group" in which to place the person. Yahoo! will send out an automatic e-mail message (which you can modify as you wish) notifying them that you have invited them to join your Messenger List. If they choose, they can add your ID to *their* list. Messenger Lists can hold up to 300 names.

When viewing your Messenger List, you'll see various symbols and messages next to the names, indicating the current status of that person. The smiley face indicates they're online, but if they haven't been active for a while, you'll also see a small clock symbol. The "sleeping face" symbol indicates that they are not currently online.

You may also see a link indicating that their Webcam is on and inviting you to view it. The numbers next to a group name show how many members are online and the total number in the group.

Sending and Receiving Messages: The IM Windows

To send a message, double-click on the person's name in your Messenger List and an IM window will pop up (see the left side of Figure 6.4). In the text entry part of that window just type your message, then hit "Send." What you send, and any replies you receive, appear in the upper box. If the intended recipient is not online, the message will be waiting for them when they log in. When you receive a message, an IM window pops up displaying the message.

Those are the basics of IM, but you can do a lot more with it. A look at the icons and menu items on an IM window will help you discover most of these additional features. The icons just above your IM text entry box lead you to some of the following options:

- **Formatting Text** – One of the simplest ways to enhance the messages you send is by formatting the text. If the Formatting Toolbar doesn't show in your IM window, click on the icon with a capital "T." This toolbar lets you add bold, italics, underlining, and color to your text and change the font face and size. Just as with a word processor, highlight the text and then, from the toolbar, click the feature you want.

- **Emoticons (Smileys)** – Place your cursor where you want the smiley to appear in the text of your message. Then click on the smiley icon and you'll see 48 emoticons (not all smiling, either) from which to choose. Click your desired smiley to insert it in your message. Your text entry box will show only the text equivalent of the smiley—e.g. :)—but the recipient will see the graphic version.

- **Audibles** – "Audibles" are smileys on steroids. Click the Audibles icon (the smiling lips) and a series of cartoon

characters will appear. Select one and you'll hear the associated message, such as "Hello, I know you're there, I can
see you!" Click "Send" at the top of the character and both
the image and the sound will be on their way to your lucky
recipient. The "More Audibles" link will lead you to dozens
of other possibilities. You may find the "Insults" category
particularly fun, though probably not in the workplace.

- **Buzz!** – Clicking the star-shaped "Buzz!" icon IMs the
word "BUZZ!!!" and a doorbell sound. Use the Buzz to
make sure your recipient notices your message, or to really
annoy them.

- **IMVironment** – Change your "IM environment" by
adding a background or sidebar to your IM window. You
can choose various themes, from Animals to Television,
plus some special IMVironments in the Yahoo! Tools category, which includes Yahoo! Photos and Yahoo! Search.
"Photos" enables you to share your Yahoo! Photos albums
at the side of the messages window. (See Chapter 9 for
more detail on Yahoo! Photos.) The Yahoo! Search
IMVironment allows someone else to see and participate
in a search you're doing. I'll discuss the Search
IMVironment later in this chapter.

The icons near the top of the IM window provide for several other
enhancements to your IM experience:

- **Webcam** – You can use your Webcam to transmit live
images to one or more people. To transmit an image, click
the Webcam icon in a message window. Your friend will
receive a message inviting them to view your Webcam. If
they accept, they'll see what your Webcam is transmitting.
When your Webcam is on, a "View my Webcam" link
appears next to your name on your friends' Messenger
Lists. When they click on that link, a message is sent to you
asking to grant them permission. You can send your
Webcam image to multiple users, including when you are in
conference mode, which will be discussed.

When you use your Webcam with Yahoo!, it ordinarily transmits at about one frame per second and with a maximum resolution of 160 X 120 pixels. If you have a broadband connection and firewalls don't interfere, you might be able to transmit in "Super" mode, which gives you 20 frames per second and a resolution of 320 X 240. That results in a clearer, much less choppy image. A link at the bottom of the Webcam window will indicate whether Super mode is an option.

- **Games –** You can play chess, checkers, backgammon, and other online games with a friend. Click on the Games icon, then on the game of your choice, and your friend will receive an invitation to play. If they accept, the game is on.

- **Voice –** Voice Chat lets you send voice messages to a friend. If you use the Conference option, you can transmit voice to more than one person at a time. You may have to disable your firewall temporarily in order for voice to work. Yahoo! provides an Audio Setup Wizard to help configure your Chat. The Wizard is available from the Messenger Help menu. To send a voice message, put your cursor over the Talk button near the bottom of the screen, hold your left mouse button down (or the Mac equivalent) and talk. Click the "hands-free" box to keep talking without holding down the button.

- **Conference –** This feature enables you to communicate by text with several people at the same time and also to use Voice Chat with each. When you click on the Conference icon, you get an "Invite Contacts to a Voice Chat" window with your Messenger List on the left. Click on the people you want to invite, holding down the Ctrl key to select several at once, then click Add. The names you select appear on the Invitee list at the right of the window. If you change your mind, use the Remove link to delete invitees. In the Messages box, you can enter a message to the people you're inviting. The Invite Others button allows you to enter the

Yahoo! IDs of people not on your Messenger List. Click Enable Voice Chat for this conference if you wish, then click Invite.

- **Send Files (and Share Files)** – The Send File icon lets you send files of up to 10 MB each directly to another person. Click Send File and a window pops up in which you can enter a file name or browse your computer for the file to send. You can also include a description of the file. On the recipient's screen, a Receive Files window pops up with a link to download.

  You can control the types of files you want to receive. In the Messenger Window, go to Preferences on the Messenger menu. Then, under File Transfer, specify to never accept files, accept only with permission, or accept all files. You can make similar decisions with regard to files you send. You can also specify default directories for files you send and receive, as well as some other related choices. If a file you send is not picked up within 48 hours, Yahoo! cancels the transfer.

  Messenger offers another method for getting files to or from another user. One of the options under Preferences > File Transfer is "Directory where others can get my files." There you can specify a directory for files you want to share. The advantage of file sharing over transferring files is that the person with whom you are sharing can view all files in that directory (maximum of 1,000) and select what they want. In the File Transfer Preferences, for privacy purposes you will of course want to very carefully consider the options offered there in terms of who can get files from you and from which directories.

  To get access to someone else's shared files from an IM window, click Contact Options on the Contact menu; then select Shared Files. In the View Shared Files window, specify the person from whom you want to get files. When you click OK, the other person sees a pop-up window in which they can approve or disapprove your request. If they approve, you see the directory they designated for sharing.

An option for sharing files outside of Messenger is the My Yahoo! Briefcase (see Chapter 3), in which you can store files that specific individuals are allowed to access. Remember, too, that Yahoo! Groups (see Chapter 4) offers a file sharing feature.

- **Photo –** The Photo icon provides two choices: Share a Yahoo! Photo Album and Send a Photo from My Computer. The latter works just like Send File, described a little earlier. The album option is one of the IMVironments I mentioned earlier. This feature lets you select one of your Yahoo! Photo albums, then message the intended recipient, who must "Accept" your offer to share your photos. Once that happens, your album appears on the right side of their IM window. Your friend can click the "player" buttons to start and stop the slideshow or go back or forward one photo at a time. Clicking on a photo's file name displays a larger image.

- **Search –** Clicking the Search icon brings up a Yahoo! Web Search box. Enter your search term(s) and the response will come back in a regular browser window.

The right side of an IM window shows two "head" icons. These are for viewing an image that you've (optionally) chosen to display when IMing, and for viewing the other person's image. Click on the upper icon to see your friend's image. The first time you use IM, your image will be blank. Click on it, choose Share Display Image, and select the image of your own that you want. You can opt to not share your image at all, share it with your current contact, or share it with everyone. You can also create an "Avatar," a cartoon character to represent you. Just click on "Create your own Avatar" and follow the instructions.

At the very top of an IM window are several menus: Conversation, Edit, View, Contact, and Help. Many of the commands on those menus are either obvious or duplicate what you can do with the icons I've already described. If you prefer to use keyboard commands rather than pointing and clicking, the menus list some keyboard shortcuts. But these menus offer some additional options and features you might find useful:

- **Conversation > Save as** – Saves, as a text file, the text portion of the messages in the current window.

- **Conversation > Print** – Prints the text portion of the messages in the current window.

- **Conversation > Preferences** – The preferences here actually apply not just to conversations, but to all aspects of Messenger. You can opt to automatically launch Messenger, enable sounds for "events" such as alerts, choose colors and skins for Messenger windows, archive messages, alerts and conferences; change your display image, filter chat text, configure your connection with regard to firewalls and proxies, change the tabs on your main Messenger window, set permissions and locations for file transfers, specify users whose IMs you want to ignore, edit your settings for LAUNCHcast Radio, configure your message window display; alter your "privacy" settings to appear "invisible" to your contacts, show your Webcam availability and set various Webcam options and permissions. If you find yourself transmitting IMs prematurely by hitting Enter, or you want to format your messages more neatly, consider changing the "Pressing Enter in a message window" option to "inserts a carriage return."

- **View** – Allows you to display or hide the Conversation, Audibles, and Text Format Toolbars, as well as your Display Image. Also lets you time-stamp messages and—assuming you've turned on "archiving" via the Conversation > Preferences menu—look at your "Recent History" of conversations .

- **Contact > Contact Options > Ignore User** – Instructs Messenger to ignore communications from a particular user. To ignore someone on your contact list, you have to delete him or her first.

- **Contact > Contact Options > Stealth Settings** - Use this when you want to indicate that you're offline (even when you're not), or to display your status as offline to a particular user.

- **Contact > Contact Options > Contact Details** – Changes the details of your Yahoo! Profile.
- **Contact > Contact Options > Message Archive** – If you have enabled Archiving (under Preferences), this takes you to your message archive.
- **Contact > Contact Options > Shared Files** – Initiates a request to see another user's files (as discussed earlier in this chapter).
- **Contact > Contact Options > View Webcam** – Turns on your Webcam.
- **Contact > Send a Text Message** – Enables you to send a text message to someone's cell phone. Enter the phone number and your message. That's it. You can enter up to 152 characters. It's a lot easier than keying in messages on your own phone. Currently you can only send messages to Verizon Wireless, Cingular, and AT&T Wireless phones, plus phones from several non-U.S. carriers.
- **Contact > Other menu options** – Most of these options are obvious and/or were already covered. They include sending e-mail via IM, placing an Internet phone call (for which you need a Net2Phone account), Buzz, Voice Chat, and inviting others to view your Webcam, play a game, or participate in a conference.
- **Contact > Send a File** – Transfers a file, as discussed at length earlier in this chapter.
- **Help** – Don't hesitate to check out the help screens when you're exploring a feature. Yahoo! has done a good job of keeping them brief but informative.

A Closer Look at the Main Messenger Window

The first window you see after signing in is the main Yahoo! Messenger window (see the right side of Figure 6.4). The four menu items at the top—Messenger, View, Contacts, and Help—provide access to most Messenger features, but the two tabs near the top, Messenger and Address Book, and the icons there, give quick access to the most-used functions.

Messenger Tab

With the Messenger tab selected (this is the default view) you see your Messenger List in the main portion of the window. Your contacts are arranged in groups. The groups you see initially are Other and Yahoo! Help. The latter provides automated assistance in using Messenger. You can create new groups by clicking Contacts, then Edit Messenger List, and finally Create New Group. You can move contacts by dragging their name to the appropriate group.

Beside each contact you'll see a symbol indicating whether they are online (smiley face) or offline (sleepy face), and a link if their Webcam is broadcasting.

Address Book Tab

Click the Address Book tab on the main Messenger window to display the contents of your Yahoo! Address Book. Each entry includes an indication of the types of contact information available—IM, cell phone, e-mail, and voice phone. Click on a name to see or edit the details for that contact. Clicking on a contact with an e-mail address produces an Invite link with which you can add them to your Messenger List.

Messenger Window Icons

Four icons are visible near the top of the window when either the Messenger or the Address Book tab is selected:

- **Add** – To add contacts.
- **IM** – Instead of double-clicking on a contact to initiate an

IM session, you can click here and, in the resulting IM window, enter the ID of the person you want to message.

- **Text** – To send a text message to a cell phone.
- **Chat** – Provides access to Yahoo! Chat Rooms (discussed in the next section).

At the bottom of the Messenger window are additional tabs/icons for LAUNCHcast Radio, Yahoo! Games, Stocks, Weather, and Calendar. Chapter 9 talks about these in more detail.

- **LAUNCHcast Radio** – Enables you to listen to radio stations provided by Yahoo!'s LAUNCHcast service, discussed in Chapter 9.
- **Games** – To play games online with other users.
- **Stocks** – Displays quotes for portfolios you set up in My Yahoo! or Yahoo!'s Finance section. The Edit link allows you to edit your portfolio. For more information, see Chapter 8, Yahoo! Finance.
- **Weather** – Displays weather reports you select here, in My Yahoo!, or in the Yahoo! Weather section. See Chapter 9 for more details.
- **Calendar** – Allows access to your Yahoo! Calendar (see Chapter 3).

The down arrow to the right of these icons brings up a Customize window that allows you to remove any of them and/or add icons for News, Sports, and a "Yahoo! Overview." News and Sports provide the content of those modules from your My Yahoo! page. Yahoo! Overview is a compilation of links to your personalized sections of Yahoo! such as Mail, Personals, Calendar, and Stocks.

Searching the Web Through Messenger

You can get to a Web search box by clicking on the Search icon at the top of any IM window. However, the Yahoo! Search IMVironment lets you perform a search jointly with another person anywhere in the world (see Figure 6.5). This feature should interest you particularly if you teach searching or help others search the

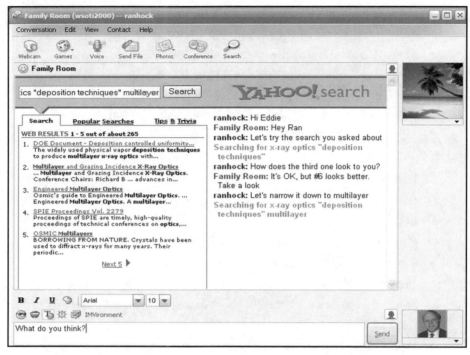

Figure 6.5 Yahoo! Search IMVironment

Web. To search through Messenger, click the IMVironment icon above the text box on any IM window. Choose "See All IMVironments," then Yahoo! Tools. There you'll find the Yahoo! Search feature. You can also get there from your browser by going to: tools.search.yahoo.com/messenger/imv/search.html. (Mac users don't have access to IMVironments at the present time.)

If you are not already messaging with your intended search "partner," you can enter their Yahoo! ID in the To: box at the top of the screen, then enter your terms in the search box and hit Search. The other person will see the results at the same time you do. Either of you can click on an item and it will open up in a separate window on that person's screen. The other person will see a pop-up message indicating what item was clicked on. Either person can enter a new search or modify the current one. There is no Advanced Search page, but you can use all the advanced techniques, such as prefixes, that you can use on Yahoo!'s main search page. (See Chapter 2 for details of searching the Web with Yahoo!.)

CHAT

The concept behind chat is excellent. Theoretically, you can go online, find a chat room devoted to a subject that interests you, settle in and ask questions, get input, share your views, debate and discuss issues with people all over the world. If you have a computer hardware problem, you could describe it and get good, sound advice, in real time, that'll help you solve it. In reality, you might want to put Chat pretty low on your priority list. With some digging and some luck, you *could* run into some people who have intelligent and useful things to say. Statistically, though, you're more likely to encounter world-class jerks who apparently have nothing intelligent to say about anything, especially the topic to which the chat room is ostensibly dedicated. (A lot of analogies could be developed between Yahoo!'s public chat rooms and public restrooms, but we'll just give that a miss.) Yes, worthwhile chat rooms do exist, with very nice and helpful people in them, but they're hard to find.

If you do have the patience to explore the utility of chat rooms, here are a few basics to help get you started. To get to Yahoo! Chat, click on Chat on Yahoo!'s main page or go to chat.yahoo.com. On the left of the page you'll find browseable categories (see Figure 6.6). Click on a category for a list of chat rooms in that category. The listings in the directory are primarily "Yahoo! Rooms" set up by Yahoo!. User Rooms also exist, but you get to them through a different route.

Very popular chat rooms sometimes have multiple "rooms." Each one displays the number of people currently in the room, how many have voice chat enabled, and how many have Webcams enabled. Click on a room and the Chat software loads. Click on a Continue button if you see one. You are now in the chat room; you'll see a list of current participants on the right, and messages in the larger window on the left. To send a message, type it in the text entry box

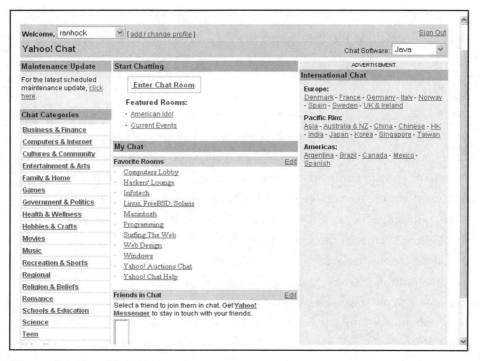

Figure 6.6 Chat Main Page

beneath the current messages. You can use the formatting toolbar to style your text. If you have enabled Voice Chat, you'll see a Talk button and volume controls for your speakers.

Depending on the version of Chat you're using (it varies with your Web browser), you'll find buttons or links that allow you to Change Rooms, go to "User Rooms," and create your own room. To create your own room, you give it a name, describe the topic, and decide whether you want it to be Public Access, Private (not listed), or Secured (participants must first be invited). You also specify whether to allow Voice Chat.

To chat with friends, acquaintances, and colleagues, you might find it easier, more pleasant, and more productive to use Yahoo! Messenger for individuals and Messenger's Conference option for multiperson conversations. If you want to chat with people you don't know, consider using Yahoo! Groups and setting up a group devoted to your specific topic. You can enable "Chat" for your group and have access to all the Chat features. But you'll also have some degree of control over who can participate in the group and the nature of the conversation. Plus, Yahoo! Groups offer a lot of nifty features that regular Yahoo! Chat does not. (Learn all about Yahoo! Groups in Chapter 4.)

MESSAGE BOARDS

Yahoo! Message Boards are another place to post and read messages, but not in real time as with Messenger and Chat. Although you may have to wait a while for a response to something you posted, an advantage (probably) of Message Boards is that the messages are left there and don't disappear almost immediately, as happens with Messenger and Chat. You can easily browse through messages and search their content. In general, Message Board conversations tend to be much more substantive and thoughtful than what you find in Chat. Yahoo!'s Message Boards are somewhat downplayed; they've even lost their place on Yahoo!'s main page. To get to Message Boards, you must first click on "More Yahoo! Services" or "All Y! Services" on the main page and find it on the long alphabetical list of Yahoo! offerings, or go directly to messages.yahoo.com.

The main Message Boards page has both a search box and a directory, enabling you to easily find boards and messages of interest. The directory is very similar to Yahoo!'s Web directory in both appearance and structure. The top-level categories are basically the same as the categories in Yahoo! Chat. You usually have to click down two to three levels to get to actual messages, for example, Family & Home > Genealogy > By Location. Once there, you'll see a list of message "threads." A thread is a series of connected messages comprising the original message on a specific topic, the replies to that message, replies to replies, and so on. The list of message threads shows the subject, the total number of messages, and the date of the last post. Click on a thread to see the first message in the thread.

Each message displays the Yahoo! ID of the person who posted it, and the date and time it was posted. When reading a message, you'll see links for navigating to the first, last, previous, or next message in the thread, or to a specific message number. A Reply link enables you to post a response.

In addition to browsing categories for boards that might interest you, you can search for specific content using the search box on the main page and on most other Message Board pages. Terms you enter are searched not just against the Message Board category headings but also in message subject headers and the actual message text. Multiple search terms are ANDed together (see Chapter 2 for more about AND), and terms are automatically "stemmed." For example, a search on *manchu* will automatically get *Manchurian*, too. You can use quotation marks to specify an exact phrase: "lawn fertilizer." Use the Options link next to the search box on the main page, or the radio buttons on other Message Board pages, to limit your search to the subject line, the poster, or the message text itself.

The Options links near the top of Message Board pages allow you to turn Yahoo!'s "Profanity Filter" on and off, specify the filter level as Weak or Strong, mask profanity with "#"s or hide those messages entirely, and turn the "ignore user" feature on or off. An Ignore User link appears adjacent to every message you read. If you don't want to see any further messages from that person, click the "ignore" link. If someone is truly obnoxious—meaning threatening or libelous, not just tasteless—you can use the Report Abuse link to call that person to Yahoo! management's attention.

An easy way to track Message Board discussions is to add the Message Board module to your My Yahoo! Page. Then use the "Edit" link to display new messages from the boards you select.

You'll also find message boards in various other parts of Yahoo!. For instance, the news sections feature discussion boards for news stories, and individual stock pages within Yahoo! Finance include message boards for that company.

GeoCities

GeoCities is a site on which you can build and store your own Web sites for free. GeoCities started out as an independent company, but was purchased by Yahoo! in 1999. Since then, Yahoo! has integrated it more and more into the rest of its offerings. Because building Web pages is outside the major thrust of this book, and because space here doesn't allow adequate coverage of what GeoCities can do and what you can do with GeoCities, I won't go into great detail. It should be mentioned, though, since GeoCities is indeed part of Yahoo!'s "communications" function.

Having a Web site of your own on GeoCities is indeed free. The catch is that the free version comes with ads, but they're relatively unobtrusive. For a small monthly fee, you can get rid of them. GeoCities provides three different ways to build your site and provides an extensive collection of features that can easily be added to your page.

Your Yahoo! ID and password are all you need to create a GeoCities Web site. You'll have to answer a few additional questions when you sign up for GeoCities but, other than that, you're all set.

To actually build your site, you have your choice of three approaches:

- Create your Web pages elsewhere, either from scratch or with a Web authoring program such as DreamWeaver or Front Page. Then upload them to GeoCities using either the Easy Upload or File Manager feature.
- Use Yahoo! Page Wizards, which offer templates and a step-by-step process to customize and make the page your own.
- Use Yahoo! PageBuilder (see Figure 6.7), in which you start out with blank pages and, piece by piece, put together the elements you want on your pages: text, links, images, backgrounds, horizontal lines, buttons, bullets, and other HTML features. On top of that, you can add news headlines, weather reports, a Yahoo! search box, maps, driving directions, stock quotes, a guest book, counter, and forms for surveys and other purposes.

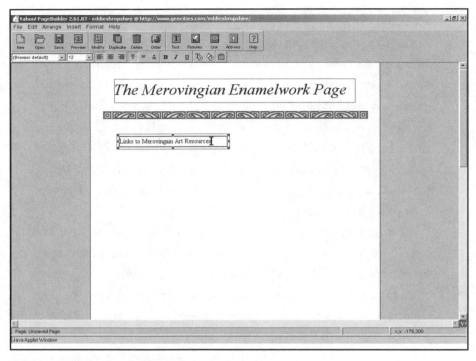

Figure 6.7 Yahoo! PageBuilder

If you've never had a Web site of your own, Yahoo! GeoCities is an excellent place to start.

A GREAT COLLECTION OF COMMUNICATION TOOLS

As this chapter demonstrates, Yahoo! gives you a variety of ways to communicate—from e-mail and instant messaging, to chat rooms and message boards, to creating your own Web site. And don't forget Yahoo! Groups, discussed extensively in Chapter 4. Explore! Try out each of the venues described in this chapter, and decide for yourself which best suit your needs.

CHAPTER 7

Buying and Selling Through Yahoo!

One of the many activities Yahoo! makes easier is spending your money. When you're on Yahoo!, you're never far from a link that will help you purchase something. If you're really serious about shopping, this is your chapter. We'll look at a wide range of areas within Yahoo! that focus specifically on that adventure. From the other direction, if you're in business to sell things, or it's finally time to get rid of that priceless family heirloom that you never could find a place for, Yahoo! will make your life easier as well.

Apart from the ads you'll encounter throughout Yahoo!, there are three main places to check out when you're in a shopping mood or looking to purchase something in particular: Yahoo! Shopping, Yahoo! Classifieds, and Yahoo! Auctions. You'll find some opportunities elsewhere to spend money as well, but they usually tie into one of these three.

YAHOO! SHOPPING

Yahoo! Shopping is the main showcase for Yahoo!'s product database. The database includes millions of products from more than 17,000 affiliated merchants plus items and merchants that Yahoo! has identified on the Web. That means that if a product is for sale online, Yahoo! will probably know about it.

Yahoo! gives you three quick and easy approaches to the products

159

database:

- Click on the Shopping link on the main Yahoo! page
- Go to shopping.yahoo.com
- Click on the Products tab above the search box on Yahoo!'s main page, enter one or more terms, and click the Yahoo! Search button

The first two avenues take you to the main shopping page where you can search for a specific item or browse by category (see Figure 7.1). From there, you go to a product listing page. The third way, searching from Yahoo!'s main page, takes you directly to a list of matching products, but you bypass some useful options.

Yahoo! Shopping Main Page

The main page for Yahoo! Shopping (shopping.yahoo.com) has the same familiar look as Yahoo!'s main page: a search box and a browseable directory. The page also offers an advanced shopping search option, a list of most popular product searches, product

Figure 7.1 Yahoo! Shopping Main Page

reviews, a link to My Saved Products, the ability to Shop by Store and Shop by Brand, a general Web search option, a link to Yahoo! Auctions, various "help" links, and featured products (another name for ads). Next to the search box is a pull-down window enabling you to limit your search to one of the top-level product directory categories.

Browsing Yahoo!'s Product Directory

The product directory, labeled Browse, enables you to browse through 18 product categories. As with other Yahoo! directories, clicking on a category takes you to more specific subcategory pages, and eventually to a product listing page. Browsing is especially useful if you don't know what terminology might be used to describe a particular product, or you're not quite sure what you're looking for. Think of it as Yahoo!'s equivalent of window-shopping.

Product Category Pages

Category pages vary somewhat depending on the product. All pages, though, have navigation tabs to go to other top-level categories and subcategories, a more detailed list of subcategories, and featured products and sponsored links (ads) specific to the category. There's also a search box and a pull-down window for searching "All of Shopping" or within the current category only.

Category pages also provide different features unique to the type of product. For example, the Automotive page includes an Auto Parts Finder, the Computers page might list the most popular laptops, Music might rank the top albums, and so on. Some offer Yahoo!'s SmartSort feature, which will be discussed later. Some pages provide shopping advice, such as "How to buy a digital camera," and product reviews, particularly from *PC World* and *Consumer Reports*.

The subcategories on the left side of the page are *selected* popular subcategories, not a complete list. For example, under Sports, you might see a Camping and Outdoors subcategory, with three further subcategories under that. But you must click on Camping and Outdoors to see the Boating subcategory.

Product Listings via the Directory Approach

Once you've browsed your way to a product listing page you'll discover a number of features to make your shopping easier (see Figure 7.2). Depending on the product, these might include links to more specific subcategories, and a keyword search box for narrowing your results even further. At this point, for instance, you might restrict your search to a specific product feature or characteristic. A Sort window lets you sort by price, instead of the default sort by Top Matches.

For each product listed, you'll generally see, in addition to the name of the product, a brief description, the price, and the store that carries it. Clicking on the product name takes you either to a price comparison page or out of Yahoo! and to the store's Web site, where you actually purchase the item.

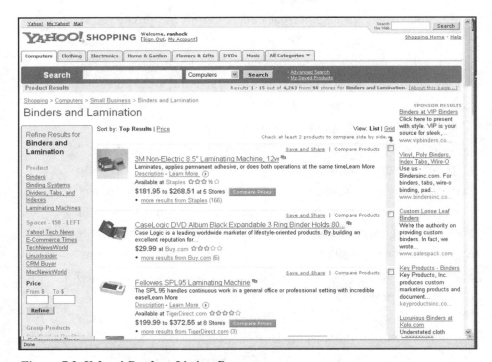

Figure 7.2 Yahoo! Product Listing Page

A typical product listing page also includes the following:

- **Merchant rating** – One to five stars indicating average user opinions. Ratings display only for merchants with at least five ratings. Ratings by customers who have actually purchased online and filled out a survey are weighted twice as heavily. Click on the stars, which indicate overall rating, to see detailed ratings for five categories: Price, Shipping Options, Delivery, Ease of Purchase, and Customer Service.

- **Review This Merchant** – Enables you to rate the merchant and, if you wish, write a review.

- **My Saved Products** – You can gather information about products in which you're interested and decide later what you want to buy. On your My Saved Products page you can sort by product name, price, date added, or category. You can also add your own notes about the product, do a side-by-side comparison, remove individual items, or make your purchase. You can also e-mail the page and, of course, print out a printer-friendly version.

- **More Results from This Store** – Shows other products in the same category offered by this merchant. The number tells you how many additional products are available.

- **Compare Checked Products** – Most categories include a checkbox next to individual items. Click on the ones that interest you, then click this link for a side-by-side comparison of the selected products. The charts compare prices, merchant ratings, and shipping costs (to your own ZIP code or another one). You can sort the chart by any of those criteria.

Certain categories—Books, Computer, Electronics, Movies & DVD, Music, and Video Games—are product- rather than merchant-oriented. Instead of specific prices and merchant information, you'll usually see:

- User ratings for the particular product
- Price range for all merchants that carry the item
- A price comparison chart similar to the Compare Checked Products listing previously described

Some categories differ in what they display on product listing pages. For example, when browsing the Computer category, instead of a keyword search box for narrowing your search, you'll often see a detailed set of boxes, called "Finders," to the left of the item listing. These allow you to narrow your results by manufacturer, licensing type, pricing level, system, media format, interface, and so on, depending on the kind of product. Product-oriented categories may also offer a more extensive list of sort options.

SmartSort

Some category pages include a SmartSort option. This is a powerful way to compare a selection of products according to several criteria, automatically sorting them based on how you weight those criteria. On the SmartSort page you first specify your preferred price range. Yahoo! presents you with a list of additional criteria, each of which has a "slider" next to it. For PDAs, for example, the criteria are Installed Memory, Display Size, Special Features, Brand, and Compact Size. Some criteria, such as Special Features, include a list of specific elements or aspects of the product. You move the slider to the left or right according to the relative importance you assign to that criterion, from "not important" to "most important." As you move the sliders, your list is automatically reordered, with the highest conforming product at the top.

Shop by Store and Shop by Brand

If you know the store or the brand you prefer, use the Shop by Store or Shop by Brand option on the main Shopping page and elsewhere in Yahoo! Shopping. Shop by Store provides an alphabetic index to nearly 233,000 (at this count) stores, as well as listings by product category. You can elect to see only stores with, say, a five-star rating. Shop by Brand also gives you an alphabetical and a categorized listing.

Searching for Products

So far, we've focused on the Yahoo! Shopping Directory and using it to browse for what you want to buy. The other main approach, and one that you might prefer, is searching the product database. If you know exactly what you're after, "search" might be better than "browsing." You can search the Yahoo! products database from the main shopping page, from most other pages on Yahoo! Shopping, from the main Yahoo! page and the Yahoo! Search page (search.yahoo.com) by selecting the Products tab, and from the Yahoo! Companion toolbar (pull down the window next to "Search").

No matter where you are on the Yahoo! Shopping site, you'll probably find a search box near the top of the page, with a pull-down window that allows you to search the entire product database, or a particular category. You'll also find a link to the Advanced Search page (see Figure 7.1).

Yahoo! automatically ANDs together the words that you enter in the search box, meaning that all words must be present in a product description for it to be retrieved. You can also use an OR to indicate that records can contain either or both (or any or all) of your search terms. A minus sign in front of a word will exclude items that contain that word. For example, to eliminate printer *cartridges* from your search for a certain brand of printer, you might enter:

hp OR lexmark inkjet printer -cartridge

You can use quotation marks to specify a phrase. The Yahoo! shopping search engine ignores capitalization, as well as some common words, such as "the."

On the main shopping page, the window next to the search box allows you to search within a specific category. Some categories, such as Computers and Office, are combined here. Category searching is a very good way to deal with terms that are used in the context of different and unrelated products. For example, to find albums for the group "The Explosion," you can eliminate a lot of books, software, and companies with the word "explosion" in their name by searching for the word "explosion" and limiting your search to the "Music" category.

Advanced Product Searching

The Advanced Search link allows you to do simple Boolean operations ("all of these words," "any of these words," "none of these words") and to specify a phrase (see Chapter 2 for more about Boolean searching).Yes, you can do all this in the main search box, but here you just fill in the forms. You can also limit your results to a particular product category, as you can in the basic search box. The Advanced Search page does let you limit by price range, though you can do the same thing on a product search results page. Bottom line: Using the Advanced Search option is a matter of personal preference; you can usually get the same results faster by using the main search box.

Search Results Pages

The product listings you see as a result of a search are similar but not identical to the results you see when browsing (see Figure 7.3). Individual product descriptions are the same, but there will be a set of "Also try . . ." links at the top of the page showing other searches that might help you focus your query.

Depending on the product, you may see other, more specialized options as well. For example, if you search for "laptops," you get the option to narrow your results by price, manufacturer, processor type, and other characteristics. As when browsing through Yahoo!'s Shopping center, you'll also be treated to "Sponsor Results" related to the products you searched for. Remember that, in categories that list items by store rather than by product, only one item from each store is shown. You can click on "more results from..." to see additional matching items.

"My Orders," "Shopping Carts," and Yahoo! Wallet

For most of your shopping selections, you leave Yahoo! behind and go directly to the merchant's site to complete your transaction. But when you buy from a Yahoo! affiliate merchant, as opposed to a store site found by Yahoo!'s product crawler, the merchants provide their shopping cart and order information to Yahoo!. At many points during your Yahoo! Shopping sojourn, you'll see links to

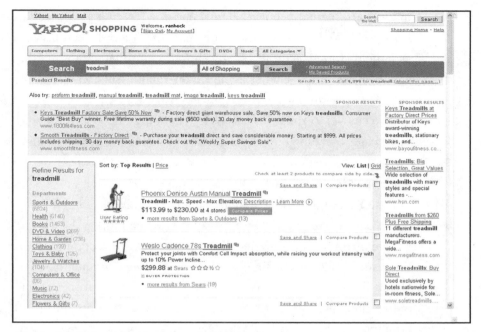

Figure 7.3 Yahoo! Product Search Results Page

"My Orders" and "Shopping Carts." Here you will find your accumulated orders and shopping cart information from Yahoo! affiliate merchants.

When you check out from the Yahoo! Shopping Cart page, you'll be asked to verify your Yahoo! Security Key, unless you've done so recently. If you haven't yet established a Security Key, you can do so at this point. The first time you purchase through Yahoo!, your credit card and shipping information is stored in your "Yahoo! Wallet," so you don't have to reenter that data when purchasing through other Yahoo! services such as Shopping, Travel, and Auctions.

YAHOO! AUCTIONS

If you're shopping for something not found in a regular store, something old, or something new, perhaps something blue (sorry, no borrowed things), try Yahoo! Auctions. Here you will, indeed, find a tremendous variety of items, some sold by "stores," but many by individuals, regular people with just one or a few or a garage-full of stuff to sell. You can be on the selling end, too. Yahoo! Auctions isn't as large or varied as eBay, but you'll find items that aren't on eBay and, because of the smaller audience on Yahoo! Auctions, you may be able to get similar items at a lower cost.

You can get to Yahoo! Auctions by clicking Auctions on Yahoo!'s main page, by going directly to auctions.yahoo.com, or by installing the Auctions button on your Yahoo! Companion Toolbar or the Auctions Module on your My Yahoo! page.

Like Yahoo! Shopping, Yahoo!'s main Auctions page has a familiar layout: A search box (with Advanced Search link) at the top and a topic directory for browsing. The Getting Started section contains links for Quick Tour, Sign up, Site Map, and Community. The Quick Tour is particularly useful if you haven't participated in online auctions; novices will feel much more comfortable about jumping in. Sign Up and Site Map are for just what they imply. Community offers Message Board and newsletter options that auction regulars may find useful. The main page also features "spotlighted" and "showcased" items that are, in effect, ads.

Browsing for Items

When you select a category on the main Auctions page, you typically see a page with subcategories, "spotlighted" items for that category, featured items, and other ads. The search box at the top allows you to do a general search throughout Yahoo! auctions or just within the current category. Clicking on a subcategory yields a listing of specific items. Yahoo! shows 25 items per page.

Once you get to this level, you can limit your browsing results to auctions that "Have a photo," "Were listed today," "Have no reserve price," "Have a buy price," or "Accept PayPal." To specify one or more of these, click the appropriate checkboxes, then click "Update."

You also have the option to view both photos and text for each item (the default), text only, or photos only. Click on a column heading to sort the list by title, price, bids, and time left for the auction. The arrows next to Price and Time Left let you sort in ascending or descending order.

For each item you'll see:

- **The title, or name of the item** – Clicking on the name or photo takes you to the Item Page with details about the seller, the item, bidding information and history, and the link to place a bid.

- **A photo, if supplied** – A larger image, as well as additional photos, may be available on the Item Page.

- **Price** – Supplies the current highest bid.

- **Time** – Supplies the amount of time left before the auction ends.

- **Auction details** – These may include:

  - **"No Reserve"** – The seller has not specified a minimum selling price.

  - **"Buy Now" and "Buy Price"** – The seller is willing to bypass the bidding process and sell the item at a specified price immediately.

  - **"New"** – Auction started within the last 24 hours.

  - **Seller** – Clicking on the seller name takes you to the seller's page, which lists other items they're currently selling, their ratings on past transactions, their closed (previous) auctions, and additional information if provided by the seller. You can contact the seller at any point for clarification or more detail about the item you're interested in.

  - **Seller's rating** – A score based on the total number of positive minus negative ratings. Click on the score for transaction details and buyer comments.

  - **Types of payment accepted** – The seller may choose to accept cash, checks, money orders, credit cards, or online payment through PayPal. To use PayPal, you must have established a PayPal account at paypal.com.

The Item Page offers some additional features as well. You can add an item to your Watchlist, which enables you to keep track of bidding. You can add the auction closing date to your Yahoo! Calendar, e-mail information about a particular auction to others who might be interested, or use Neighborhood Watch to alert Yahoo! management if you think the item is inappropriate for an auction.

Searching for Items

You may prefer to use the search box to locate auction items, especially if you're not sure of their category, or if you know specifically what you're looking for. Terms you enter in the search box are automatically ANDed. Although the search documentation claims that you can use quotation marks to search for a phrase, as you can elsewhere in Yahoo!, my experience is that they are ignored. You can, however, use a minus in front of a word to eliminate it from your search:

baltimore   -orioles

The pull-down window next to the search box allows you to limit your search to one of the main auction categories. Your terms will be searched against the name of the item and the words in its category.

Advanced Search mode lets you refine your search by price range, buy price, category, or location (within 5 to 250 miles of a specific ZIP code or U.S. city and state). You can also narrow your search to auctions that have met their reserve price, or have no reserve, or accept PayPal.

Search results appear almost identical to the items listings you see when browsing. At the top of the page, however, Yahoo! displays any categories that contain your search term and a list of the main categories with a link to matching items in that category. You can also opt to Save Your Search and review/rerun your saved ("Favorite") searches. You can also set up an e-mail alert by entering a simple search and specifying how frequently you want the results delivered.

Bidding and Buying

Bidding is easy, but first you have to register for Yahoo! Auctions, which you'll be asked to do the first time you click to bid on an item. If you already have a Yahoo! ID, registering for Auctions is very quick. Once registered, you'll find a Place a Bid window on item pages. When placing your bid, you also specify whether you want Yahoo! to "Bid up to this amount on my behalf," otherwise known as automatic bidding, or "Bid this exact amount," known as straight bidding. In automatic bidding, your bid will be raised automatically, by the amount of the minimum bid increment, each time someone outbids you, until your maximum bid is reached or the auction ends. The bidding increments are based on the starting price of the item.

Shortly after you place your bid (unless you were immediately outbid) you'll receive an e-mail message confirming the bid, describing the auction, and providing help links for further details and information. You'll also be notified when you've been outbid, when you've won an auction, and so on. The Options link lets you specify additional events you want to be notified about, and the notification method—e-mail, Yahoo! Messenger, pager. The Options page also allows you to change your profile, set auction alerts, create a blacklist of sellers with whom you don't want to do business, etc.

There are a number of variations on the bidding process. Sellers may set a reserve, or minimum, selling price. If that price is not met, the seller does not have to sell. Sellers may also end an auction early if the bidding reaches an amount that they feel is adequate. A bidder may purchase an item immediately by meeting that "Buy Price." The seller may have activated an option to automatically extend the auction by five minutes if a bid is placed during the last five minutes of the auction. This helps cut down on the practice of "sniping," in which bidders miss out because someone else who has been tracking the auction all along emerges to outbid them in the last few seconds. When you've won a bid, the seller will contact you with payment and shipping instructions and options.

If you haven't participated in online auctions, spend some time browsing through the Yahoo! Auctions help screens before you place your first bid. The system offers plenty of built-in protections, such as seller feedback and ratings, but you'll feel much more comfortable with the process if you know what to expect.

Selling Items

Yahoo! Auctions provides an easy and inexpensive way to market and sell your wares or just unload those odds and ends in your "yard sale" pile. You can sell a single item or thousands of them—though if you really want to go into business, a Yahoo! Store, discussed below, may be a better option.

The best way to get started in selling is to familiarize yourself, first, with Yahoo! auctions from the buyer's point of view. Spend some time browsing though Yahoo! Auctions to get a good feel for how it works. You might even place a trial bid or two on items you wouldn't mind owning. Then, click on the Selling Stuff link on the main Yahoo! Auctions page, take the Selling Tour featured there, and check out Yahoo!'s help links, suggestions, and documentation for sellers. Finally, just jump in and list an item or two.

Here's a quick overview of the steps involved in selling through Yahoo! Auctions:

- **Choose a category for your item** – First, browse through the current auctions to see where similar items are listed. When you click on Sell Stuff, the first screen will walk you through your category and subcategory choices.
- **Describe the item and name your price** – After you choose the category, Yahoo! will lead you to the page where you describe the item, upload photos (up to three), set the starting price, the length (2–10 days) of your auction and its start and close times, specify a reserve price (optional), the payment options you will accept, whether you or the buyer will pay for shipping, and when you will ship (upon close of the auction or upon receipt of payment). You also get to

choose promotional options, such as "featuring" your items and highlighting, all for a fee.

- **Preview your listing** – You have a chance at this point to make changes.

- **Sit back and wait for the money to pour in** – In the meantime you may get questions from potential buyers, and you can track bidding on your My Auctions page.

Yahoo! provides sellers with numerous other options, including "bulk loading" of items, editing items after the auction has started, closing an auction early, rating bidders, and others. Even if you don't plan to sell through Yahoo! Auctions on a regular basis, it can be interesting to try. You might even make a little money.

CLASSIFIEDS

Yahoo!'s Classifieds are yet another alternative for buying and selling online. The biggest difference between Classifieds and Auctions is that the items listed in Classifieds are all at fixed prices. Note, however, the use of the phrase "Asking Price" in many listings, which implies a potential for bargaining. The categories also differ from other Yahoo! Shopping venues, as do the searching capabilities.

You won't find certain kinds of items on Yahoo! Classifieds because their sale is forbidden. Some are obvious, such as fireworks and other explosives, body parts, illegal or stolen goods, and "hate" items. Some things, however, can't be sold through Classifieds because their sale would conflict with Yahoo!'s other offerings, such as travel and financial services, and event tickets. You can't sell your massage or psychic services or employment contracts, either. Yahoo!'s Classifieds help screens provide a full list of no-no's.

The main Yahoo! Classifieds page consists principally of a list of categories, a Quick Search area where you can search within categories, and the My Classifieds section, where you can track ads you've posted and access ads and searches you have saved. A Featured Listings section highlights ads for which the owner has paid an additional fee. Links at the top of the page enable you to

post an ad or take a "Tour" of Classifieds, which is not nearly as useful or necessary as the Auction Tours (see Figure 7.4).

The Classifieds categories are: Used Cars, Real Estate, Tickets,
Pets, Air & Watercraft, HotJobs, Rentals & Roommates,
Merchandise, and Personals. All sections have a search feature that
allows you to search the listings. Some categories—Tickets, Pets,
Air & Watercraft, and Merchandise—include a Browse Listings or
similar option for looking through subcategories. Other sections,
though, take you out of Yahoo! Classifieds and into another section
of Yahoo!—to pages that, in the early days of the Web, might have
been referred to as "channels." Now you might recognize them as
specialized "portals." Autos, HotJobs, Pets, Tickets, and Personals
all take you to the corresponding Yahoo! section. Real Estate and
Rentals and Roommates both take you to Yahoo! Real Estate. Each
of these sections has a number of resources relevant to that topic.
For example, the Yahoo! Real Estate page has resources (as well as
ads) for mortgages and financing, moving, insurance, researching

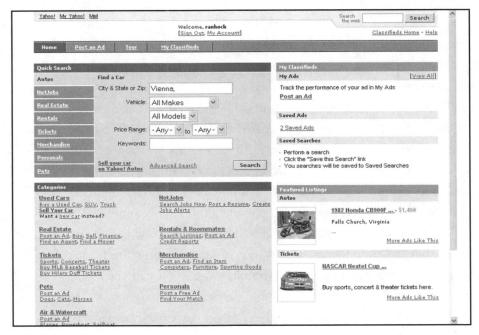

Figure 7.4 Main Yahoo! Classifieds Screen

schools and neighborhoods, real estate news, and other tools. The best way to understand what these sections offer is simply to spend some time browsing there. You will undoubtedly discover a number of specialized and useful surprises.

You can search Classifieds from either the main Classifieds page or any of the section pages. On the main page is the Quick Search area from which you choose one of the categories (except, strangely, the Air & Watercraft section) and do a search. The search options are category-specific. For example, in Autos, you can search by location, vehicle, model, price range, and keywords. For Tickets, you search by price range, event date, and keywords. Each Quick Search offers an Advanced Search link with further criteria. You may see somewhat different search options when you click one of the category or subcategory headings elsewhere on the main page. Many categories offer a choice of searching "locally," narrowing your search Yellow Pages–style. Some allow you to set up an "alert," whereby you'll be notified when new listings come up that match your search criteria. Depending on the category, search results pages might include options to save your search, to sort results by date, price and category, or to change the location covered by your search.

When looking at Classifieds, you'll notice links such as "Reply to this Ad," "Save this Ad," or "E-mail Ad to a Friend." The reply option enables you to contact the merchant to purchase or to ask questions. "Save" allows you to accumulate ads of interest for later viewing and decision making. The main Classifieds page includes a link to your saved ads.

To place a classified ad, click on one of the "Post an ad" links on the main page or elsewhere in Classifieds. The process is very similar to listing an item in Yahoo! Auctions. You choose a category, enter details including pricing, and provide billing information. As with auctions, you can opt for a number of additional options and features, including adding a photo, seeing statistics on performance of your listing (daily figures on how many times the ad was viewed), and making changes to your ad at any times. "Bulk" sellers who submit at least 100 unique ads per week can use a .csv (comma separated values) format to upload them. Posting an ad costs less than $10 and runs for 21 days.

If you're in a shopping mood, consider looking in Yahoo! Classifieds. You may find items that you won't pick up on the Shopping page or in an auction.

YAHOO! STORES

Yahoo! claims to host "one in eight online stores." Yahoo! Small Business (smallbusiness.yahoo.com) will demonstrate how you can take advantage of a variety of Web hosting plans, "Merchant Solutions," and other Yahoo! products and services that can provide you easily with a storefront on the Web. Many of these features are similar to those offered by other Web hosting services, but Yahoo!'s are unique in that you can tie into Yahoo! Shopping, and have a huge potential marketplace and an immediate "store" presence online.

A FINAL WORD ON SHOPPING

Given the range of products and services—essential, nice-to-have, and just plain fun—that you can tap into on Yahoo!, it's safe to say that you have the opportunity to buy and sell like you've never bought and sold before. And all without leaving your chair. Yahoo! Shopping, Yahoo! Auctions, Yahoo! Classifieds, and Yahoo! Stores all have their selling points, so to speak, whichever end of the transaction you're on.

CHAPTER 8

Yahoo! Finance

Yahoo! Finance is largely investment-oriented. Unless investing, or just following the financial markets, occupies a sizeable portion of your attention, Yahoo! Finance is unlikely to thrill you. On the other hand, the Finance section has such a broad range of resources and features, including consumer finance and money management tools, that parts of it should interest you even if you're not a serious investor. In fact, if you want to learn more about financial instruments, markets, and the workings of Wall Street, Yahoo! Finance has a *lot* to offer.

A substantial amount of information appears right on the Yahoo! Finance home page. However, that page also includes more than a dozen prominent links to what Yahoo! refers to as Centers—Today's Markets, Stock Research, Financial News, and so on. The amount of information you'll discover once you get into these Centers dwarfs what you find on the home page. Most of the content in Yahoo! Finance, on the home page, and in the Centers, falls into the categories of news, data, advice, tools, and services. Many of these are free, some carry a price tag, and others are a combination of "free" and "fee."

YAHOO! FINANCE HOME PAGE

The first time you look at the Yahoo! Finance home page (see Figure 8.1), you may find it a bit overwhelming. It features a very broad range of tools, services, and other resources, many of which are interconnected in various ways. But, as suggested elsewhere in this book, spend a little time exploring the page and you'll develop a much better feel for what it offers. Also, the assumption throughout this chapter is that you have signed up for a Yahoo! account. Some of the content discussed in this chapter won't be visible to you unless you have an account and are signed in.

Figure 8.1 Yahoo! Finance Home Page

Though the actual arrangement changes occasionally, you usually see the following sections on the Yahoo! Finance home page:

- Your **"personal" links for Services, Accounts, and Portfolios**
- The **Quotes Search** box
- **Icons for major or featured sections of Yahoo! Finance**: Mutual Funds, Bill Pay, Banking, Loans, Insurance, Planning
- **Market Summary –** Provides a quick look at the current

picture, the day's change and percent change for major U.S. market indices and stocks. Use the Edit button to select which ones you want to follow.

- **Financial News and Featured Articles** – News stories from the Yahoo! Financial News Center, with feature articles drawn from various Finance Centers.
- **My Recent Quotes** – Quotes for stocks and indices you have selected.
- Links to the various **Yahoo! Finance Centers**, including Today's Markets, Stock Research, Financial News, and Industries.

The pages that follow will go into detail about these sections and Centers, and the resources to which they lead, beginning with Quote Search and then each of the Yahoo! Finance Centers. The "personal links" are covered toward the end of this chapter, along with Yahoo! Finance's other "Personal" offerings.

QUOTE SEARCH

The most prominent search box on the Yahoo! Finance home page lets you search for stock quotations and related information. The same search facility is also available on My Yahoo!'s Portfolios module (see Chapter 3). You can enter up to 50 ticker symbols, separated by commas. If you don't know a company's symbol, click the Symbol Lookup link next to the search box. Then enter the name of the company (or a portion of the name), choose the Type (Stocks, EFT, Options, Mutual Funds, Indices), and the Market (U.S. & Canada, or World Markets), and click Look Up. On the Look Up results page, just click the symbol you're looking for. Quotes are supplied by Reuters and cover more than 50 worldwide exchanges. Nasdaq quotes are delayed 15 minutes and other exchanges 20 minutes. The Yahoo! Finance premium service gets you real-time quotes.

The results for a quote search include last trade, trade time, change, previous close, open, bid, ask, and other standard data, an intraday price chart, and links to related news headlines (see Figure 8.2). For most U.S. stocks, you'll also find links to additional information: Options, Historical Prices, Technical Analysis, Company Events, SEC Filings, Competitors, Analyst Coverage, Analyst Opinion, Analyst Estimates, Research Reports, Major Holders, Insider Transactions, Roster, Income Statement, Balance Sheet, Cash Flow, and others, including a Message Board. These in turn may lead to additional helpful information. For example, if you click on a name in the Insider Roster, you'll get a list of other companies with which the person is connected.

Figure 8.2 Yahoo! Finance Quotes Page

YAHOO! FINANCE CENTERS

Links on the Yahoo! Finance home page lead you to a variety of "Centers" devoted to particular aspects of investment and personal finance. The type of information offered differs considerably depending on the focus of the Center. Some Centers include a

Customize link that lets you choose your news headline sources, the default brokerage(s) for quotes pages, and various other settings.

Today's Markets

The Today's Markets section of Yahoo! Finance provides a large collection of data regarding the day's market activities. The search box here, and also in the Stock Research section, allows you to specify the information you want: Basic data, DayWatch, Performance, Real-Time Market, Detailed, Chart, Research, Options, or Order Book.

Links in this section take you to detailed, in-depth content from Briefing.com, Reuters, and other sources:

- **For the NYSE and Nasdaq**, number of advances, declines, and unchanged; up, down, and unchanged volumes; new highs and lows. Click "more" for the same types of data for other U.S. indices.
- **A textual Market Update** with an overview and an update every half-hour throughout the market day.
- **In Play** – Brief news reports throughout the day regarding specific stocks, such as earnings reports. Ticker symbols are linked to Yahoo!'s pages for particular stocks. (This is also available as a module on My Yahoo!; see Chapter 3.)
- **Story Stocks** – Reports of moves and the reasons behind them.
- **Today's Events** – Earnings reports, investor conference calls, economic statistics, IPOs, Splits, and Upgrades/ Downgrades.
- **Market Statistics** – Advances and Declines, Most Actives, U.S. and World Indices, Exchange Rates, including a currency converter for 150 currencies. (This is available as a module on My Yahoo!; see Chapter 3.)
- **Financial News** – Top Stories, U.S. Markets, Most Viewed Articles, Full Coverage (business news from Yahoo! News).
- **Investing Tools > Stock Market Toolbar** – This is a part of the Yahoo! Toolbar.

- **Investing Tools > Stock Alerts** – Be notified via e-mail or your mobile device when a stock you're tracking moves through the limit you specify, or get hourly price updates. Stock quotes are delayed 15 minutes for Nasdaq and 20 minutes for other exchanges.
- **Investing Tools > News Alerts** – Delivers Keyword Alerts, Breaking News Alerts, or News Bulletins.
- **Premium Services** – Real Time Quotes, Research Reports, Premium News. You'll need to pay for these; free trial periods are often available.

Stock Research

Whereas the Today's Markets section focuses, naturally enough, on what's happening now, the Stock Research section of Yahoo! Finance emphasizes overviews, analysis, and background. In this section you'll find:

- **Company Earnings** – Earnings reports list for the day, with links to listen to the archived recording, Quarterly Earnings Surprises list, Conference Calls schedule for the day.
- **Analyst Research** – Report Screener (search for reports on a particular company by analyst firm, author, and date), Analyst Performance Center (see how well a particular analyst actually does), Analyst Recommendations, Upgrades and Downgrades, Sector and Industry performance data (this is sortable online, and can be downloaded to a spreadsheet). This data is available as a module on My Yahoo!.
- **Company Reports** – Free downloadable annual reports, SEC filings, and financial statements.
- **Mutual Funds, Bonds, and Stocks** – Links to other Yahoo! Finance Centers (covered later in this chapter).
- **Financial Calendars** – Stock Splits, economic statistics, IPOs, Mergers.
- **Research Tools** – Stock Screeners, including a Java applet that enables you to screen by more than 150 criteria, view

tables and histograms, and save results to a portfolio or export to a spreadsheet; Mutual Fund and Bond Screeners, Historical Quotes (also downloadable to a spreadsheet).

Financial News

This section draws on the broader resources of Yahoo! News (see Chapter 5). The Financial News page displays financial headlines and stories from Reuters (these are also available in the Headlines module on My Yahoo!). You also get a financial news directory that allows you to browse stories by broad categories such as U.S. Markets, Economy & Government, and by categories and subcategories in certain areas.

Industries

The Industry Center provides news, data, and reports by industry and sector. The main Industry Center page includes:

- **Today's Top Performing Industry** – Includes links to a detailed industry page and related stories.
- **Today's Industry Highlight** – Five top-performing and five worst industries.
- **Featured Industry Profile from Hoover's Online.**
- **Locate Industry by Company** – Enter a ticker symbol in the search box to see the Industry Center for the sector in which the company is classified.
- **Leaders & Laggards** – As measured by highest dividend yield, market capitalization, P/E ratio, return on equity, and revenue growth.
- **Top Industries** – An alphabetic list of links to the Industry Centers for top industries. Click Complete Industry List for a full listing.

Education

The Education section contains an extensive collection of resources for understanding finance and financial markets. It's not "everything you need to know," but it goes a long way. The education page includes:

- **Investing 101** – Articles from SmartMoney.com and Investorama.com on getting started in investing, choosing a broker, understanding stocks, options, etc.
- **Financial Dictionaries** – Online dictionaries and glossaries for finance, bonds, insurance, options, and taxes.
- **Personal Finance 101** – Articles on the basics of banking from Bankrate.com and on insurance, loans, managing debt, real estate, retirement, and taxes from a variety of sources.
- **Finance Bookstore** – Links to books available from Yahoo! Shopping.
- **Finance Quiz** – 50 online finance quizzes.
- **Web Sites** – Links to relevant sections of the Yahoo! Web Directory.

Mutual Funds

The Mutual Funds Center contains:

- **Fund Lookup** – In the first search box, you can enter a fund symbol and go to the Quote page for that fund. In the second, you can enter a symbol to identify the fund and see its Quotes page.
- **Fund Screener** – Allows you to search for funds by 17 criteria.
- **Top Performers** – A directory of funds that you can browse by sector, style, and strategy.
- **Prospectus Finder** – Links to prospectuses that you can download.
- **Exchange Traded Funds** – Links to the ETF Center (discussed later).
- **Inside Mutual Funds Education** – Featured articles on mutual funds.
- **Latest News** – Funds-related headlines and stories.
- **Tools** – Screener, lists, calculators for comparing funds,

determining when to sell, analyzing fee structures, etc., plus Morningstar editorials and message boards.

- **Education** – Articles on understanding and investing in mutual funds.

Exchange-Traded Funds (ETFs)

The Exchange-Traded Funds Center contains:

- **ETF Lookup** – Enter an ETF symbol in the first search box and go to the Quote page for that fund. Enter a symbol in the second search box to identify the fund by name and go to the Quotes page for that fund.
- **ETF Browser** – Search by category and fund family, view charts showing return, trading/volume, holdings, risk, and operations. Click the column heading to sort by a particular data item.
- **ETF Education** – Articles on what ETFs are, how they work, and links to news stories.
- **More on ETFs** – View ETFs (links to the ETF Browser charts), ETF News and Commentary, and Glossary.
- **Other Tools** – Mutual fund tools and related links from the Yahoo! Web Directory.
- **Top Performing ETFs** – Intraday price performance numbers for the leaders.
- **View All ETFs** – Takes you to the ETF Browser.

Bonds

The Bond Center includes data from ValuBond on 12,000 secondary bond offerings. This section includes:

- **Bond Lookup** – Search by bond name.
- **Composite Bond Rates** – Graphs and charts for U.S Treasury, Municipal, and Corporate Bonds.
- **Market Summary** – New issues, commentary, analysis. (Available as a module on My Yahoo!.)

- **Bond Screener** – Search for bonds by type and seven other criteria.
- **Bond Calculators** – Determine the best bonds to buy, price to pay, when to sell, etc.
- **Bonds 101** – Articles providing an introduction to bonds, bond types, and bond strategies.
- **Latest Bond News from Reuters.**

Options

The Options Center provides:

- **Options Lookup** – Enter a stock symbol to get Call and Put Options prices for the current and next five months.
- **Options Analysis Tool** – Enter a stock symbol in the search box, then select a sentiment (Bullish, Bearish, Neutral), an implied volatility (high or low), an option strategy (e.g., Buy Call), and a sort preference; you get a chart of top-ranked trades that match your criteria.
- **Most Actives** – A chart of the previous day's high-volume stock options.
- **Options 101** – Articles on investing in options.
- **Options Glossary** – A glossary of more than 250 options-related terms.
- **Option Dragon** – Based on volume, ratios and/or volatility, find matching stocks and their options.
- **Options News** – Options headlines from the past several days.
- **Expirations Calendar** – Identifies dates on which various types of options expire.
- **Options Message Boards** – Yahoo! Messages Boards covering Futures and Options.
- **Resources** – Links to related Yahoo! Finance sections and tools.
- **Web Sites** – Links to relevant sections of the Yahoo! Web Directory.

Community

The Yahoo! Finance Community section provides links to Yahoo!'s Business and Finance Message Boards, Chat Rooms, and Groups that focus on investing.

International

Yahoo!'s International Finance Center is divided into four sections:

- **World Markets** – Click on a continent, then a country, to get a Country Profile supplied by CountryWatch.com. This includes a country Fact Sheet and narrative background on the country's economy and environment.
- **Latest International News** – Financial headlines from Reuters.
- **Related Resources** – The Yahoo! Currency Converter, Major World Indices, and International News (more detailed access to international financial news from Reuters).
- **World Finance** – Leads to a Finance section of the "local" Yahoo!'s for more than 20 countries. You will find that each of these local Yahoo!s looks at least somewhat similar to the Finance section of Yahoo!'s U.S. version, but is in the language of the country and with other variations appropriate to that country.

YAHOO! PERSONAL FINANCE CENTERS

Yahoo! offers eight Personal Finance Centers: Bill Pay, Money Matters with Suze Orman, Banking, Credit Reports, Loans, Insurance, Planning, and Taxes. In addition, there is one more personal finance tool, Yahoo!'s Portfolio, which deserves at least as much attention as any of the Yahoo! Finance offerings. (This is the same portfolio feature that is available as a module on My Yahoo!.) Links to the eight centers are found on the lower left portion of the main Finance page and the portfolio link is found near the top of the page.

Some of these services require submitting credit card and/or bank account information, Social Security number, and other personal information. Yahoo! has partnered with reputable organizations to provide these services, and you're probably safer entrusting them with your private information than you are giving your credit card to a restaurant waiter you've never seen before. However, you should exercise reasonable caution, especially if you use a laptop or share your computer with someone else. Think twice before clicking to "Save your password." Fortunately, access to the more sensitive areas of Yahoo! Personal Finance requires an additional "Security Key."

The personal finance features appear, for the most part, near the Top of the Yahoo! Finance Page. Yahoo! does move them around from time to time, so if you don't find them there, look elsewhere on the page or use the Finance Search box to locate them.

Portfolios

With Yahoo!'s Portfolios, you can not only track stock prices, mutual funds, and indices, but add your own investment data, such as number of shares held and initial price. That means that you can quickly determine the value of individual holdings and of your total portfolio. (Be aware that Nasdaq quotes shown in your portfolios are delayed 15 minutes, and quotes from other exchanges are delayed 20 minutes. Real-time quotes are available as a Premium Service). You can maintain as many Yahoo! portfolios as you wish. Links at the top of the Yahoo! Finance home page allow you to create new portfolios, edit existing ones, and hide your portfolio information from casual passers-by. You can also include your portfolios as a module on your My Yahoo! page. The "add brokerage" link allows you to add your brokerage account information for use with Yahoo! Money Manager, discussed a little later in this chapter.

To set up a new portfolio, click Create a New Portfolio. You can then specify the issues you want to track and the information to display. The portfolio views that Yahoo! creates will vary depending on your choice. To track your current holdings, for example, enter the appropriate stock symbols, select any market indices you also want to follow, determine how you want them sorted, whether you want to display the portfolio value in My Yahoo!, and which of several items to include: shares owned, purchase price per share, trade date, commissions, upper limit, lower limit, notes. You then input the number of shares, price per share, and other data, depending on the item. Your completed portfolio enables you to see, at a glance, its total value, value change, and gain (see Figure 8.3).

You can also choose to display a variety of "views," such as Basic, DayWatch, Performance, Real-Time Market, and Detailed. Each shows various data in addition to the items you selected when you created the portfolio. Most views can be edited to add or delete data items. Altogether you can select from more than 80

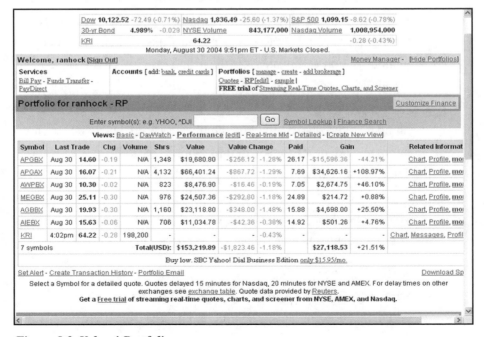

Figure 8.3 Yahoo! Portfolio

data elements. You can also set up alerts, create a transaction history, and have an updated copy of the portfolio e-mailed to you daily.

Clicking on a stock symbol in your portfolio displays a detailed Quotes Page for that stock. You can also link to recent news stories for the stocks you have included.

The Download Spreadsheet link allows you to automatically download selected data from your portfolio, typically ticker symbol, last price, date, time, change, open price, daily high, daily low, and volume.

Bill Pay

Yahoo!'s Bill Pay feature is provided by CheckFree and is similar to online bill payment services offered by banks and elsewhere. Bill Pay is also available as a module on My Yahoo!. In addition to viewing and paying bills, you can get e-mail reminders when bills are due, create regularly scheduled automatic payments, project cash flow, and review your payment histories. You can receive bills from 85 payees and pay bills online to more than 100 payees. The Premium plan lets you receive bills from more than 200 payees. If the company you want to pay is not on Yahoo!'s list, you can add it manually. For companies on the list, you can view not just the amount due, but also an image of the bill itself.

To sign up for Bill Pay, you'll need to supply your Social Security number, your driver's license number, birth date, address, phone number, and other personal information, as well as the Routing Transit Number and account number shown on your checks. Your data will be verified by Equifax Credit Information Services. Once you've enrolled, you set up your list of payees, and then determine your payment schedule, request reminders, etc.

Money Matters with Suze Orman

This section contains brief articles and tips from TV celebrity and author, Suze Orman.

Banking

The Yahoo! Finance Banking Center primarily includes links that enable you to find current rates for various types of loans and investments. In addition, you will find links to services already discussed, such as Bill Pay, and a variety of learning resources related to personal credit and banking:

- **Savings Finder** – For credit cards, long-distance calling, and checking accounts, the Savings Finder provides a form where you characterize your account usage. Savings Finder checks this against various providers and plans, and gives a price comparison for the ones that best match your needs.

- **Learn More** – A collection of brief articles providing advice and information in categories such as Bank Accounts and Services, Managing Credit Cards, Online Banking, Managing Your Credit Rating, Banking Safely, and Online Bill Payment.

- **Find a Bank** – Choose a metropolitan area and Find a Bank comes up with a chart showing major banks in that region, with a comparison of user ratings, checking account costs and fees, monthly fee waiver levels, and interest checking rates.

- **Savings Rates** – Charts comparing National Savings Rates for CDs and Rates by Institution.

- **Home Equity Rates** – Home Equity Loan Rates by metropolitan area and state.

- **Auto Loan Rates** – Auto loan rates for new and used cars at the national, state, and metropolitan area levels.

- **Calculators** – Specialized calculators for managing credit cards, credit lines, IRAs, and savings. For example, "What will it take to pay off my balance?" or "How large a line of credit can I obtain?"

Loan Center

The Loan Center offers:

- **Mortgage Center** – Current rates, mortgage calculators, articles and headlines on mortgages.

- **Auto Loan Center –** Rates by type of loan, region, and institution; calculators for assessing loans and leases; articles on buying cars, and links to related resources in other Centers.
- **Articles and links to other Centers and resources** on mortgages and other types of loans.

Insurance

The Insurance Center includes sections on Auto, Health, Life, and Home and Renters Insurance. These sections offer quotes from a variety of insurance companies, articles, tips, and calculators.

Planning

The Planning section is, for the most part, an aggregation of planning-related tools found elsewhere in Yahoo! Finance. These include Savings Finder, Bill Pay, Credit Reports, and Finance Planner. The Planning Center does, however, include a substantial collection of articles containing background information and advice on financial planning.

Taxes

The strength of the Yahoo! Tax Center is *education*. It features a collection of guides, articles, tips, and links to other resources within Yahoo! and elsewhere on the Internet, such as the IRS. The Tax Center also contains a good selection of links to federal and state tax forms, and tools such as Tax Calculators, a Tax Prep Checklist, Tax Calendar, Tax Rates, and Tax Glossary. You can go directly to the Tax Center at taxes.yahoo.com.

GETTING THE "MAX" FROM YAHOO! FINANCE

One characteristic of Yahoo! Finance is the extent to which its offerings are also available elsewhere within Yahoo!. To get the maximum benefit and efficiency from Yahoo!'s finance-related offerings, consider how and where you want them delivered. Many Finance offerings give you three main options: your "My Yahoo!" main page, the My Finances page in My Yahoo!, and the Yahoo! Finance home page.

If finance is of major interest to you, you might want to go directly to Yahoo! Finance a great deal of the time. Even in that case, however, think about putting some Finance modules, such as your personalized portfolios, Company News, and Market Summary, on your My Yahoo! page. That can be especially handy if you've made My Yahoo! your "start" page.

As an alternative, remember that you can set up multiple My Yahoo! pages and access them easily from your main My Yahoo! page. One of the preset pages is My Finances, which incorporates most of the personal finance options and can be customized to meet your needs.

Also keep in mind that the Yahoo! Companion Toolbar provides a Finance Companion Toolbar option, which features a Quote Search box and buttons that lead directly to the various Finance Centers and to your portfolios. No matter where you are on the Web, you're only a couple of clicks away from Yahoo! Finance and its broad range of resources.

CHAPTER 9

Other Seriously Useful Yahoo! Stuff

This chapter is about the rest of Yahoo!. Chances are good that you'll never stop discovering useful facets and corners of this rich and complex site. When you think you've mastered it all, new features and enhancements will come along to pique your interest. Chapter 1 touched briefly on the best-known and most likely useful parts of Yahoo!. Some came up again, in passing, later in the book. Chapters 2 through 8 focused in more detail on the areas where serious users are likely to spend most of their Yahoo! time. But some Yahoo! features and services deserve more attention than was given in Chapter 1, though not necessarily a chapter of their own. Addressing those is what this chapter is about. You can get to any of the following Yahoo! sections from links on Yahoo!'s home page.

INTERNATIONAL YAHOO!

Yahoo!'s main page at yahoo.com is U.S.-centric. Its language is English, and it's aimed primarily at the needs and interests of users in the 50 United States. But that doesn't mean that Yahoo! has forgotten the rest of the world. In fact, Yahoo! has set up sites for Denmark, France, Germany, Italy, Norway, Spain, Sweden, the U.K. and Ireland, Australia and New Zealand, China, Hong Kong, India, Japan, Korea, Singapore, Taiwan, Argentina, Brazil, Canada, and

Mexico. There's also a Yahoo! aimed at Asia in general. In addition to those region-specific sites, Yahoo! offers a site in Catalan, as well as versions for Chinese and Spanish speakers in the U.S. You can get to these international Yahoo!s from the bottom of the main Yahoo! page, by visiting world.yahoo.com, or by going directly to fr.yahoo.com, de.yahoo.com, or whatever the address might be.

The home page for most International Yahoo! sites is laid out very much like the U.S. version, with parallel but not identical content. For non-English speaking countries, the page is written in the language of the country. The search box features familiar tabs for alternate databases such as Images, the Web Directory, and News. But you probably won't see a Products tab or a Yellow Pages tab (although, elsewhere on the page, you might find a link to a local Yellow Pages). Beneath the search box is the option to restrict your search to the language and/or the country of the site. The ads on the page pertain to the region and, in fact, the content of the site is not just a translation of the U.S. version. The German site, for instance (see Figure 9.1), features German news, sports, stocks, weather, and TV. International Yahoo! doesn't just pay lip service to the "world wide" Web. Yahoo! has indeed gone "native."

U.S. City Guides

As well as expanding beyond its U.S. site, Yahoo! has gone "local" in the other direction by providing city guides for metropolitan regions throughout the U.S. You can find the City Guides either by going to cityguides.local.yahoo.com or by typing the city's name into the Yahoo! search box and then looking for the "Local City Guide" link above the regular search results. These guides represent a combination of selected Yahoo! features (Yellow Pages, Maps and Driving Directions, city Web sites from the Yahoo! Directory) and services provided by Citysearch.com. The Citysearch portion of City Guides pages includes:

- **Search Citysearch** – Enter a type of business or activity, such as French restaurant, park, concert, or golf, and get a

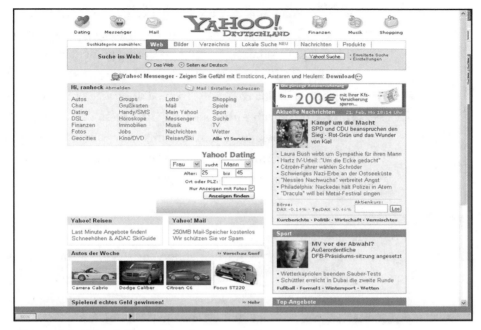

Figure 9.1 Yahoo! Deutschland

list of matches in your vicinity. Each entry includes the name of the place or event, the distance from your location, and a rating. You can sort the list by rating or distance. Click on the name of an entry and, depending on the type of search, you might also see links for making reservations or buying tickets, or to a map and directions to the venue, special offers, or the organization's Web site.

From the Citysearch results pages, you can modify your search, changing terms and locations. You'll also find a Saved Locations window with an Edit/Change link that enables you to maintain a list of places, such as favorite vacation spots or cities you travel to regularly on business, so you don't have to key in the coordinates every time you do a search.

- **Browse Citysearch** – Links adjacent to the Citysearch search box enable you to browse by category: Tickets &

Events, Restaurants & Bars, or Spa & Beauty. The Tickets & Events link leads to browseable subcategories. You can also choose a subcategory and specify a particular date or date range. In Restaurant & Bars, you can browse by type of cuisine, and in Spa & Beauty, by type of service or treatment.

- **Other Citysearch options** – The Citysearch section of the City Guides includes additional links for dining, lodging, and other attractions. An Events Calendar lets you click on a particular date to see a list of events.

TRAVEL

If you use Travelocity for travel planning, especially airline reservations, portions of the Yahoo! Travel section (travel.yahoo.com) may look familiar, since Travelocity is Yahoo!'s main provider of travel services (see Figure 9.2). However, Yahoo! has integrated additional features and content that add significantly to Yahoo! Travel's value. These include Alerts and Travel Updates, among others. The featured options on Yahoo! Travel appear in tabs or links at the top of the page: Travel Guides, Flights, Hotels, Cars, Vacation Packages, Cruises, Deals, and My Travel. With a few exceptions, such as some vacation packages, you can book your flight, rental car, hotel, and other trip requirements online through Yahoo! Travel. If you have questions or run into problems, you can contact a real, live person at Yahoo! Travel by phone. Though the "reservations" pages (flights, hotels, cruises, etc.) focus on searching, each one also presents unique offerings. The ads on these pages can actually be quite helpful when you're looking for travel bargains.

The Search box on the Travel page enables you to search the entire Travel section. Results typically lead you to the relevant sections of Yahoo! Travel and to specific portions of the Yahoo! Travel Guides.

The Yahoo! Travel page also includes two other major features: **Quick search** and **Travel Guides**. Quick search enables you to search for Flights, Hotels, Cars, Vacations, Cruises, and Deals. Each category lets you specify your basic criteria as well as additional

Figure 9.2 Yahoo! Travel

options. The More Options links take you to the same page you would get to by clicking on the equivalent major tab near the top of the Travel page.

Yahoo! Travel Guides are both extensive (covering 17,000 cities throughout the world, 80,000 hotels, and 140,000 "things to do") and deep, with a broad variety of information about accommodations and attractions in each city they cover. Click on the Travel Guides tab to get to specific travel guides. You can either click on a map to specify the area you want, or use the Browse Travel Guides directory. The latter includes links for major destination countries and areas only, so if you want to visit Slovenia (as you should), use the map and start by clicking on Europe. The Travel Guides page also spotlights a particular city, with a map, a slideshow, and selected links for "the best of" what the city has to offer. In addition, you can access Yahoo! Interest Guides, which focus on particular activities and places such as national parks, skiing, and beaches.

Additional links for selected attractions, cities, and hotels appear at the bottom of the page.

What you will typically find in the Travel Guide for a major city can best be understood through an example. If you look at Paris, you'll get a brief paragraph describing the city with a Read More link leading to a somewhat more detailed description. A photo and associated slideshow gives you a visual impression of the city. For Paris, you'll see more than 50 color photos. The page also displays today's temperature; click on it for a full Parisian weather forecast from Yahoo! Weather.

You'll really appreciate the robust content of the Travel Guides when you click on the tabs at the top of the page: Hotel Guide, Things to Do, Entertainment, Restaurants, Shopping, and Maps. Selected links for each of these categories also appear on the main page for Paris. Don't miss the collection of links to "Sites We Like," which include a variety of city-specific resources covering tours, reviews, articles, guides, maps, and transportation.

Click on the Hotel Guide tab for a list of almost 800 Parisian hotels. You can sort the listing alphabetically by name, or by popularity or price. You can also select by name, price range, or type (hotel, condominium, historic, resort, pension, etc.). For each hotel, you get a brief description, the average price per room (the average for the Hotel Meurice is $637), the user rating (1–5 stars), plus links to reviews and to add your own rating. Click on the name of the hotel for more information and a link to make a reservation through Yahoo! Travel.

The Travel Guide Things to Do tab typically leads to descriptions of sights, activities, and attractions. For Paris, you get 196 listings, though there are certainly more things than that to do in Paris. You can sort the list alphabetically or by popularity, or browse by category or name. Choose the Musée Rodin and you'll find a description, an image of The Kiss, the phone number, a link to the museum's Web site, opening hours, nearest metro station, user rating, reviews, and a link to a Yahoo! image search for the museum.

The Entertainment link on the Things to Do page will help you decide whether you want to spend the evening at the Moulin Rouge, listen to poetry at the Lapin Agile, or choose from the other 170 venues listed. Each listing includes specific information similar to what you get for Things to Do.

Use the Restaurants tab for information on 165 places to eat in Paris. Again, you can sort by general price, or browse by name, type of cuisine, atmosphere, or neighborhood. You can determine, for instance, that Maxim's accepts major credit cards, but is not open on Sundays.

The Shopping link on the Things To Do page provides a somewhat sparser collection of choices, with 45 places to spend your Euros. By the way, Au Printemps is open on Thursdays until 10 P.M.

The Map tab on the Travel Guide for Paris leads to a map that covers only the area most frequented by tourists, so you may want to do a Yahoo! search for "Paris maps" to locate more comprehensive maps.

The Travel Guides on Yahoo! Travel definitely qualify for the advice given back in Chapter 1—*Click everywhere.* The more you poke around here, the more good things you'll discover.

At the bottom of the main Yahoo! Travel page are links to International Yahoo! Travel Sites. Each of these region- or language-specific Yahoo! Travel pages provide information parallel in content and structure to Yahoo!'s U.S. Travel section.

Though it was not yet appearing on the Yahoo! Travel page when this book went to press, there is another Yahoo! Travel service that may make your travel planning easier and your trip less expensive— FareChase. If you do not find it on the Yahoo! Travel page, go to it directly at farechase.yahoo.com.

FareChase allows you to simultaneously search dozens of air, car, and hotel reservation sites and easily compare prices. On the FareChase screen you will see tabs for searching Flights, Hotels, or Cars. Choose the appropriate tab and then fill out the form for departure and destination cities, check-in and check-out dates, etc., depending on which of the three tabs you choose. Click the Search button and you will see a report of progress as FareChase scours the various sites.

FareChase results are arranged by lowest price (except for a "featured result" that may appear above that list). Links allow you to sort instead by other criteria such as departure times or return times. Other parts of the results page allow you to change your specifications and then repeat the search. When you click on one of the results you are taken out of Yahoo! to the reservation site itself, where you actually make the reservation. If you are a person who typically goes to several sites to compare prices, FareChase can save you a lot of time.

MAPS

Yahoo! Maps (maps.yahoo.com) provides road maps and driving directions for specific street addresses and for businesses, either by name or by type. Coverage at present is the U.S. and Canada only. At first glimpse, Yahoo! Maps doesn't seem unique, compared to other Web sites that offer maps and driving directions. However, the results page features something you don't see on most other sites— Yahoo!'s SmartView option for placing restaurants, theaters, and dozens of other locations on the map you just requested (see Figure 9.3.) I'll say more about SmartView shortly.

To get a map when you have an address, select the Address tab on the Yahoo! Maps main page, fill out the form, and then click Get Map. You'll also see a My Locations window, for quick access to locations you have "saved," or to recently searched locations, without having to fill out the rest of the form. The Edit button allows you to delete, add, or change your list of locations.

To find a map for a business, click on the Business tab and fill out the form. Instead of entering an address, enter either the name of a business or a category (e.g., flowers). For businesses, you see a Near this Location window instead of a My Locations window.

To get driving directions, click on the Driving Directions link and fill out the forms for your starting address and your destination.

Once you have a map, you can do a number of things to "refine" it. These include:

- **Zooming** – The Zoom In - Zoom Out bar to the left of the map enables you to zoom in or out to 10 different levels. Level 8 is the state or province level; level 10 is the country level. You can also zoom in on the map just by holding your cursor over the map and clicking. Radio buttons permit you to change the default to recenter the map without zooming in.

- **Re-Center** – The eight directional arrows around the map enable you to re-orient the map, showing areas to the North, East, Northeast, and so on.

- **Make Map Larger or Smaller** – A link next to the map lets you increase or decrease its size.

- **Map Legend** – Click Map Legend for a pop-up window that provides an explanation of the various symbols and colors on the map.

- **Driving Directions** – Click on "To this location" or "From

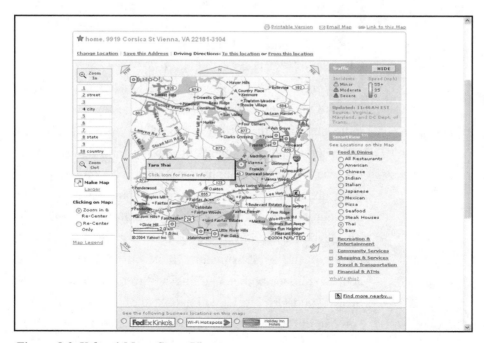

Figure 9.3 Yahoo! Maps SmartView

this location" and fill in the starting point or destination.

- **Change Location** – Use this link above the map or the Change Location form below it to generate a new map.

- **Save this Address** – Click to add the current address to your My Locations list. If you think you'll be back, save yourself the effort of re-entering the information.

- **Printable Version** – This link produces a page that's mostly "just map," without links, arrows, zoom bar, and other distractions.

- **E-mail Map** – Click to send an e-mail message with a hot link to this particular map. Very handy for sending directions to your home or a meeting location.

- **Link to this Map** – This link provides HTML code you can insert on your own Web site to produce a link to the map. Again, a handy way to direct customers or visitors to your business or facility.

- **SmartView** – Where Yahoo! Maps really stands out is in its SmartView feature (see Figure 9.3). On U.S. maps only (unfortunately), you'll see a SmartView panel with a list of categories—Food & Dining, Recreation & Entertainment, Community Services, Shopping & Services, Travel & Transportation, and Financial & ATMs. Click on any of these to get a more detailed list for that category. Click the radio button to the left of a subcategory, such as Florists, and yellow-and-red squares appear on the map indicating the location of that establishment or service on the map. If there are no matches in the current zoom-level view, the map automatically zooms out far enough to show the nearest locations. Hold your cursor over any square to see the name of the establishment. Click on a square for the address, phone number, and links to More Information, Web Search, and Driving Directions. At the bottom of the map you can opt to have the locations of selected Yahoo! advertisers, such as hotels in the area, appear on the map.

When you request driving directions from Point A to Point B, you get a map showing the route and a turn-by-turn set of driving directions. The directions also include the total distance, mileage between turns, and the estimated travel time. Use the Get Reverse Directions link to show you the way back. If you're a stickler for detail, or directionally challenged, use the Show Turn-by-Turn Maps option to get small individual maps for each turn.

When you view maps for U.S. metropolitan areas, you can see, in addition to the features just described, an overlay of real-time traffic conditions, including information on road speeds, delays, and accident reports. To see the traffic information, click on the "View Traffic on Map" button. Colored dots indicate speed conditions and triangular icons indicate traffic incidents. Green represents good conditions, yellow a minor problem, orange a moderate problem, and red a severe problem.

WEATHER

The primary function of Yahoo! Weather (weather.yahoo.com) is to show the current weather and forecasts for U.S. cities and cities throughout the world. Data is provided by the Weather Channel. You can enter a U.S. city or ZIP code in the search box, or browse by using the continent and region links.

The main Weather page does include a variety of additional features:

- **Weather News and Features** – Weather headlines from Reuters and AP.
- **Weather Video** – Links to video reports and forecasts.
- **My Weather** – Weather for cities you select by using the Edit button. This is the Weather "module" that can appear on your My Yahoo! page (see Chapter 3).
- **Inside Weather** – Links to maps and images at the U.S. Local, U.S. National, or World level. Click on any of these links to get very current satellite and Doppler radar images, forecast maps, and temperature and precipitation maps. The

Storm Center link enables you to set up Yahoo! Weather Alerts in e-mail. The Weather News link takes you to stories from the Weather Channel.

- **Featured Map** – Click on the thumbnail image to get the currently featured U.S. satellite image.
- **Full Coverage** – These links lead to press coverage from a variety of sources, of storms and other weather developments currently in the news.
- **Feature Photo** – The currently featured weather photograph.
- **Weather to Go** – Links for mobile and e-mail weather alerts, snowfall alerts, and news bulletins.

After choosing a city, you see a page displaying the current weather conditions, including present temperature, as well as high and low temperature for the day. You can select Fahrenheit or Celsius readings. You also get a five-day forecast and a link to an extended forecast. Depending on the season, you might also see links to specialized forecasts such as mosquito predictions. You'll also see more detailed current conditions such as the "feels like" temperature, barometric pressure, humidity, visibility, dewpoint, wind, and sunrise and sunset times. Another link leads to historic daily and monthly averages and records.

HEALTH

Yahoo! Health (health.yahoo.com) is a rich collection of medical and healthcare-related information, including reference works, news, and other Web-based health resources. The very real dangers of obtaining medical information on the Web are well-documented and very widely discussed. Yahoo! Health is a good starting place for research into healthcare and medical options because it's a useful, easily accessed compilation from reputable sources only. Even so, keep in mind the caveats that Yahoo! publishes at various places on the site; start by reading the fairly long one at the bottom of the main Health page. In essence, it says that the information provided is not meant for advice, diagnosis, or treatment and is no substitute for seeing a doctor. That's an oversimplification; read the actual statement at health.yahoo.com.

The search box at the top of the main Health page, and its associated pull-down window, allows you to search all Yahoo! Health or the Web. The tabs above that main search box (Healthy Living, Diseases & Conditions, Health News, Groups & Boards, Drug Guide) correspond to main sections of the page, or in the case of the fifth tab, the Drug Guide, to one of the specific tools on the page. Clicking on any of those tabs, however, will take you to a separate page, each of which is an expanded version of what you will find for that topic on the main Health page.

The Healthy Living section of the main page contains a pull-down window that leads to 17 topic pages (Health Centers) with topics ranging from Addition to Work/Life. Those topic pages are rich in resources, containing dozens of rather detailed encyclopedia-type articles, links to Related Resources (from elsewhere in Yahoo!), news, tips, and tools.

The Diseases and Conditions part of the main Health page leads to more than 30 "Health Centers" for specific diseases or health conditions. These centers contain content that is parallel to that found in the Healthy Living Centers. Spending at least a couple minutes to look at one or two of the Health Center pages is the only way to begin to appreciate the resources and knowledge available here.

Look at the Health News part of the main page for current headlines related to health and medicine. The headlines found here come from a variety of Yahoo!'s news suppliers, but predominantly from HealthDay.

The Groups and Boards section of the Health page serves as a gateway to health-related Yahoo! Groups and Message Boards.

In addition to these main sections, the Health page contains a featured topic, a poll (daily quiz), Tools (Baby Name Finder, Body Fat Calculator, Activity Finder, Target Heart Rate Calculator), and an Advice and Treatment section. Pay particular attention to the latter section, since it contains the following important resources:

- **Encyclopedia** – The encyclopedia contains thousands of health-related articles, from Aarskog Syndrome to Nightmares to Zollinger-Ellinger Syndrome. The search box at the bottom of the page enables you to search for a specific topic and the A–Z list lets you browse alphabetically. Articles provide extensive details but are written so a layperson can understand them.

- **Drug Guide** – The Drug Guide lists thousands of drugs by common, generic, and trade names. For each, it typically gives information such as Description, Proper Use, Dosing, Storage, and Precautions and Side Effects.

- **Ask The Expert** – This section provides access to well-known online medical experts, such as Alan Greene, Andrew Weil, and Donnica Moore (all MDs). You can read their answers to questions other people have sent them, and submit questions of your own.

- **Clinical Trials** – This section provides searchable or browseable access to drug studies sponsored by pharmaceutical and biotechnology companies. You can browse by subject and by state. To get detailed information on a specific trial and possibly become a participant, you must sign up with Acurian, which provides this data to Yahoo!. Sign-up is free.

PEOPLE SEARCH

People Search (people.yahoo.com) is an online "white pages" that allows you to look up U.S. and Canadian addresses and phone numbers, as well as e-mail addresses. To search for addresses and phone numbers, at least the last name is required, but you can narrow results by entering first name, city, and/or state. The results page displays (if you're lucky) the address and phone number, plus a link to automatically add the listing to your Yahoo! Address book and another link to a Yahoo! map showing the address. The links for

"Background Check " and "More Information Available" are ads for companies that provide background searches.

To search for an e-mail address, enter the person's first and last names. The results page displays (again, if you're lucky) their e-mail address. An Advanced E-mail Search option lets you narrow your search by city, state or province, country, Internet domain, old e-mail address, organization name, and organization type. Click on the SmartNames box to instruct the search engine to look for common nicknames (Lawrence/Larry, Thomas/Tom, Tommy) as well.

People Search offers you the option to add your own listing to the database, or to edit or remove it.

PHOTOS

With Yahoo! Photos (photos.yahoo.com), you can store an unlimited number of your photos online, share them with others, and have prints made. Click on the Add Photos link to create an album, choose a name for it, and you're ready to upload photos. You can either upload pictures one at a time or do it much more easily and quickly by first downloading the Yahoo! Easy Upload Tool, which takes about a minute with a high-speed connection. Using Easy Upload, you click on Select Photos, locate the folder on your computer in which your photos are stored, and then simply drag and drop one or more into the Easy Upload window. Depending on the size of your images, uploading can take longer than a minute for each one, even with a fast connection. As well as uploading photos from your computer, you can upload from your camera phone.

Once you've uploaded some photos, you'll see your albums when you go to Yahoo! Photo. Click on an album to display thumbnail images. Click on a thumbnail to see the larger image, or on Slideshow for an automated slideshow of the images in that album. You can control the slideshow by use of the player buttons, and you can also control the speed. The Edit button above the thumbnails lets you change the names of your photos, move or copy them to another album, or rearrange or delete them.

The Share an Album and Share This Album links enable you to share your photos with others. You can share an album by sending an e-mail message inviting others to view it, or you can share via Yahoo! Messenger (see Chapter 6 for how to do the latter). To share by e-mail, click on a Share link, then, in the Share by E-mail window, click on Compose E-mail. Type a message if you wish, and click Send. Your recipients will receive e-mail with a link to your album.

Yahoo! Photos also enables you to order reasonably priced prints of photos you've uploaded.

YAHOOLIGANS!

Yahooligans! (www.yahooligans.com) is a Yahoo! site designed for kids in the 7 to 12 year-old range (see Figure 9.4). It provides a directory of selected age-appropriate sites and a large collection of resources both for fun and for homework. Many teachers, as well as kids, use Yahooligans!.

Figure 9.4 Yahooligans!: The Web Guide for Kids

The Directory is very similar in overall design to the general Yahoo! Web Directory, but the categories are different:

- **Around the World**
- **Arts & Entertainment**
- **Computers & Games**
- **School Bell** – School-related categories such as Language Arts, and Math.
- **Science & Nature**
- **Sports & Recreation**

The collection of links at the left of the page provide a wide range of fun resources for kids:

- **Games** – Almost 60 games, including board and tile games, sports, knowledge, arcade, word, and card games.
- **Animals** – Don't miss the Ranger Rick Field Guides, with pictures and descriptions of hundreds of animals, including 11 kinds of flies. You'll also find animal stories, jokes, and other resources.
- **Music** – Features artists and videos of interest to this age range.
- **TV** – Not really TV, but a selection of animated videos—complete with commercials.
- **Science** – Videos, quizzes, glossaries, news and more, on topics such as space, dinosaurs, archaeology, weather, and the environment.
- **Cool Sites** – A selection of featured "cool" Web sites.
- **Movies** – Trailers and clips of new and upcoming movies.
- **E-Cards** – Send online greeting cards.
- **News** – News headlines and slideshows of interest to kids.
- **Reference** – Links to a dictionary, encyclopedia, thesaurus, almanac and other online reference tools.
- **Jokes** – Hundreds and hundreds of one-liners for kids.
- **Ask Earl** – Loads of interesting and educational questions and answers, such as "What substance in corn makes it pop?", arranged in the same categories as the Yahooligans! Directory. Kids can submit their own questions as well.

- **Horoscopes** – Horoscopes for kids.

Parents and teachers of kids in the 7-to-12 range might want to point their kids in the direction of Yahooligans!. It's fun, educational, and a safe place to spend time online.

YAHOO! MOBILE

At various points in this book, there's been discussion of Yahoo! services that are available through mobile devices such as cell phones, pagers, and PDAs. Yahoo! Mobile pulls together most of these services and gives an overview of what you can do with Yahoo! and your specific mobile device(s). Features, activation, and functionality depend to some extent on the type of device and the brand, model, and carrier. Some mobile features are free, but many involve a one-time charge or a subscription fee. To get started, click on the Mobile link on Yahoo!'s main page, or go directly to mobile.yahoo.com. Then select the service in which you're interested (Messenger, mail, Alerts, etc.), and follow the instructions.

What can you do with Yahoo! Mobile? Try some of these for starters:

- **Yahoo! Messenger** – Send and receive instant messages just as you would on your computer. The Mobile version of Yahoo! Messenger is available through most, though not all, major U.S. wireless carriers. If your carrier is not on the list but does support text messaging or Web access, you can still use a version of Yahoo! Messenger.
- **Yahoo! Mail** – If your mobile phone is Web-enabled, just sign in to Yahoo! and go to Mail.
- **Text Messages from your PC** – Send messages from your PC to anyone with a cell phone who has text messaging through a participating U.S. carrier. From the Messenger window on your PC, click "Send a text message" on the Contact menu. Then enter the phone number and your message (up to 140 characters), and click Send. It's that easy.
- **Alerts** – Get News, Weather, Stock, Sports, Auction, and

other alerts on your mobile device. You can set up your Alerts from the appropriate section of Yahoo!, such as Yahoo! News for News Alerts, or go to alerts.yahoo.com to see all the Alerts options and set up yours from there.

- **Find a Wi-Fi Hotspot –** Enter a location and find nearby wireless hotspots, as well as what they charge for access.
- **Upload Photos from your Camera Phone –** Upload photos from your mobile phone-cam to your Yahoo! Photos album. Simply e-mail your pictures from your phone to yourusername@photos.yahoo. com.
- **Photo Albums –** With a compatible color phone—not necessarily a camera phone—you can store photos in a mobile album, and create a slideshow to share with others on your phone.
- **Ringtones –** Yahoo! has an extensive collection of ringtones you can download for a fee. What a world we live in.

On mobile devices with Web access, you can also access these Yahoo! sections and services: Address Book, Calendar, Astrology, Fantasy Sports, Games, Movies, Sports, Finance, News, Weather, Driving Directions, Local Info, People Search, Restaurants, Yellow Pages, and Bookmarks. The list will probably grow longer.

LAUNCH: MUSIC ON YAHOO!

The Music link on Yahoo!'s home page takes you to LAUNCH - Music on Yahoo! (or go directly to launch.yahoo.com). LAUNCH offers customizable radio "channels," music news and videos, and information about musicians, groups, and recordings. The search box at the top of the page enables you to search all of LAUNCH or to limit your results to Artists, Albums, Songs, or Videos.

The tabs on the main LAUNCH page lead to the four major sections of LAUNCH: LAUNCHcast Radio, Music Videos, Artist, and Shop. The main page also features Music News, featured artists, albums, and videos, a Top Ten Videos list, and links to reviews, interviews, and other content.

LAUNCHcast Radio

LAUNCHcast Radio invites you to listen to your choice of genres and customize your "stations." Keep in mind that these are not AM or FM broadcasts, but on-demand music delivery. The pull-down window offers five options: Radio Station Guide, "Play My Station," "Edit My Station," LAUNCHcast Plus, and LAUNCHcast Help. LAUNCHcast Plus is a premium service that provides additional customization, premium sound quality, and other features.

The core of the Radio offerings are the Guide and the customization option. The Radio Station Guide provides a choice of music from more than 300 genres and themes in about two dozen categories. The individual genres are very specific: 1970s soft rock, Reggae Dub Zone, Garage Rock, Vintage Country, Doo Wop, Classic Vocal Standards, to name just a few. The categories are broader (Urban, Rock, Alternative, Country, Indie/Folk, 1980s, Moods, etc.) Stations with earphone symbols are ones to which you have free access. Those with plus signs require a LAUNCHcast subscription.

The Play My Station Option enables you to listen to your choice of genres and themes. You determine what you'll hear by using Edit My Station to rate individual genres, artists, albums, and songs. Your ratings can run from "Never play again" to "Can't get enough." Besides the incredible degree to which you can personalize your programming to suit your musical taste, LAUNCHcast Radio has another big advantage over broadcast stations: a pop-up window that identifies the song, artist, and album that you're currently hearing.

You can also play LAUNCHcast directly from Yahoo! Messenger.

Music Videos

When it comes to music videos, Yahoo! claims to have "The most Videos on the Web!" This part of LAUNCHcast lets you choose videos from Pop, Rock, Country, Rap, and R&B categories, or by specific artist. You can create a Video Station similar to the LAUNCHcast radio stations and edit it in a similar way.

Artists

The Artists tab enables you to view photos of a particular artist, read reviews, news, and interviews, and go to the Artist's Page and the Artist's Club. Do an Artist Search to quickly find the Artist's Page, which includes a Discography, a list of fans, perhaps a biography, and an opportunity to rate the artist.

YAHOO! DESKTOP SEARCH

So far, all of the discussion about "search" has been about searching for content on the Web. Yahoo! can also provide you with an easy, fast, and effective search of the contents of your own computer. Yahoo! Desktop Search is a free downloadable program that indexes the contents of your computer and then allows you to search that content. You can search e-mail, any Word, Excel, and PowerPoint documents, music, images, and more than 200 other file types. In using this program, you have a variety of options regarding which kinds of files get indexed. For many types of files, such as Word, Excel, PowerPoint, Adobe Acrobat, HTML, and text files, the full text of the file is indexed. For images, audio, video, and executable files (.exe and .zip), only information such as file name, file type, and size is indexed.

When you search, you can preview the results before you open the files, play audio and video content without having to first launch a separate player, and save your searches. If you wish, when you do a regular Web search, you can simultaneously search your own computer and have your "local" results appear on the same page as your Web results. With e-mail, you can go directly from e-mails you locate using Desktop Search to reply, forward, or print.

Yahoo! Desktop Search requires that you have at least Windows XP or Windows 2000 SP3 or SP4. The program is about 8 MB in size and takes about three minutes to download, using a high-speed connection. If you don't see a link on Yahoo!s main page for downloading Desktop Search, you can go directly to desktop.yahoo.com.

OTHER SERIOUSLY USEFUL STUFF

If you use Yahoo! a lot, you will surely find many more features that you can put to serious (and even nonserious) use. The variety of options, plus the level of personalization that Yahoo! makes possible, mean that no two users are likely to use it in exactly the same way. To optimize your use of Yahoo!, remember the advice given at the beginning of this book: *Click everywhere!* Keep exploring. Come to think of it, that's pretty good advice for life away from the computer, too.

CONCLUSION

Whew! That's a lot of Yahoo!. If you've read this book, or even a couple of chapters, chances are you'll agree. But think about this for a minute: The phrase "A lot of Yahoo!" actually has two meanings. Yes, we've covered a lot in the preceding nine chapters. But what you've seen is not *all* of Yahoo!—just a lot of it.

I admit that I was very subjective in deciding what to include and how much detail to provide. Yahoo! aficionados reading this book will undoubtedly ask, "Why didn't he say more about. . .?" or "Why didn't he mention the LAUNCHcast Radio option that lets me rate genres for 'my' station based on what other people I've identified like to listen to?"

Quite simply, there's more to Yahoo!—more features, subfeatures, and possibilities—than anyone could cover in a 200-page volume. Hopefully, though, I've given you a good taste of what Yahoo! can do for you.

As I remind you several times in this book, the key to "getting the max" from Yahoo! is to *explore*. Find the parts that interest you most, and then dig deeply. Bookmark your great discoveries as well as sections that you want to come back to and click around in some more. Keep fine-tuning your My Yahoo! page. And don't just stick to the "serious" stuff. There's more to Yahoo!, and there's more to life.

ABOUT THE AUTHOR

RANDOLPH E. HOCK, PH.D.

Randolph (Ran) Hock has his own company, Online Strategies, which specializes in creating and delivering customized courses on Web research. His courses have been delivered to large and small companies, government agencies, nongovernmental organizations, universities, and associations. He has trained searchers throughout the U.S. and in Austria, France, Germany, Hungary, Italy, Portugal, Spain, Switzerland, and the U.K. Ran has been a chemistry teacher and a chemistry librarian (at MIT), and was the first Data Services Librarian at the University of Pennsylvania. For many years he held training and management positions at DIALOG Information Services and Knight-Ridder Information. Ran is the author of *The Extreme Searcher's Guide to Web Search Engines* (CyberAge Books. First edition, 1999. Second edition, 2001) and *The Extreme Searcher's Internet Handbook* (CyberAge Books, 2004). He lives in Vienna, Virginia, with his wife and two younger children, loves to travel, and hopes to someday have time to again pursue his hobby of genealogy.

INDEX

More Great Books
from Information Today, Inc.

The Extreme Searcher's Internet Handbook
A Guide for the Serious Searcher

By Randolph Hock

The Extreme Searcher's Internet Handbook is the essential guide for anyone who uses the Internet for research—librarians, teachers, students, writers, business professionals, and others who need to search the Web proficiently. Award-winning writer and Internet trainer Randolph "Ran" Hock covers strategies and tools (including search engines, directories, and portals) for all major areas of Internet content.

There's something here for every Internet searcher. Readers with little to moderate searching experience will appreciate the helpful, easy-to-follow advice, while experienced searchers will discover a wealth of new ideas, techniques, and resources. Anyone who teaches the Internet will find this book indispensable.

As a reader bonus, the author maintains "The Extreme Searcher's Web Page" featuring links, updates, news, and much more. It's the ideal starting place for any Web search.

2004/296 pp/softbound/ISBN 0-910965-68-4 • $24.95

The Skeptical Business Searcher
The Information Advisor's Guide to Evaluating Web Data, Sites, and Sources

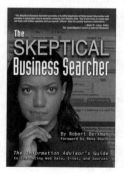

By Robert Berkman • Foreword by Reva Basch

This is the experts' guide to finding high-quality company and industry data on the free Web. Information guru Robert Berkman offers business Internet users effective strategies for identifying and evaluating no-cost online information sources, emphasizing easy-to-use techniques for recognizing bias and misinformation. You'll learn where to go for company backgrounders, sales and earnings data, SEC filings and stockholder reports, public records, market research, competitive intelligence, staff directories, executive biographies, survey/poll data, news stories, and hard-to-find information about small businesses and niche markets. The author's unique table of "Internet Information Credibility Indicators" allows readers to systematically evaluate Web site reliability. Supported by a Web page.

2004/300 pp/softbound/ISBN 0-910965-66-8 • $29.95

The Web Library
Building a World Class Personal Library with Free Web Resources

By Nicholas G. Tomaiuolo • Edited by Barbara Quint

With this remarkable, eye-opening book and its companion Web site, Nicholas G. (Nick) Tomaiuolo shows how anyone can create a comprehensive personal library using no-cost Web resources. And when Nick say "library," he's not talking about a dictionary and thesaurus on your desktop: He means a vast, rich collection of data, documents, and images that—if you follow his instructions to the letter—can rival the holdings of many traditional libraries. If you were to calculate the expense of purchasing the hundreds of print and fee-based electronic publications that are available for free with "the Web Library" you'd quickly recognize the potential of this book to save you thousands, if not millions, of dollars. (Fortunately, Nick does the calculating for you!) This is an easy-to-use guide, with chapters organized into sections corresponding to departments in a physical library. *The Web Library* provides a wealth of URLs and examples of free material you can start using right away, but best of all it offers techniques for finding and collecting new content as the Web evolves. Start building your personal Web library today!

2004/440 pp/softbound/ISBN 0-910965-67-6 • $29.95

Cashing In With Content
How Innovative Marketers Use Digital Information to Turn Browsers into Buyers

By David Meerman Scott

In failing to provide visitors with great information content, most of today's Web sites are missing a golden opportunity to create loyal customers—and leaving a fortune in new and repeat business on the table. According to Web marketing expert David Meerman Scott, too many marketers focus on style over substance. While a site may win awards for graphic design, Scott demonstrates that the key to Web marketing success is compelling content, delivered in new and surprising ways. In *Cashing In With Content*, he interviews 20 of today's most innovative Web marketers, sharing their secrets for using content to turn browsers into buyers, to encourage repeat business, and to unleash the amazing power of viral marketing. The book features a diverse range of content-savvy organizations from the worlds of e-commerce, business-to-business, and government/not-for-profit, including the Wall Street Journal Online, CARE USA, Kenyon College, Alcoa, Tourism Toronto, Weyerhaeuser, Booz Allen Hamilton, and United Parcel Service.

2005/256 pp/softbound/ISBN 0-910965-71-4 • $24.95

Web of Deception
Misinformation on the Internet

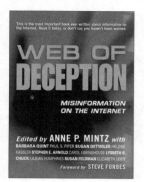

Edited by Anne P. Mintz • Foreword by Steve Forbes

Intentionally misleading or erroneous information on the Web can wreak havoc on your health, privacy, investments, business decisions, online purchases, legal affairs, and more. Until now, the breadth and significance of this growing problem for Internet users had yet to be fully explored. In *Web of Deception*, Anne P. Mintz (Director of Knowledge Management at Forbes, Inc.) brings together 10 information industry gurus to illuminate the issues and help you recognize and deal with the flood of deception and misinformation in a range of critical subject areas. A must-read for any Internet searcher who needs to evaluate online information sources and avoid Web traps.

"Experts here walk you through the risks and traps of the Web world and tell you how to avoid them or to fight back ... Anne Mintz and her collaborators have done us a genuine service."

—Steve Forbes,
from the foreword

2002/278 pp/softbound/ISBN 0-910965-60-9 • $24.95

Building and Running a Successful Research Business
A Guide for the Independent Information Professional

By Mary Ellen Bates • Edited by Reva Basch

This is the handbook every aspiring independent information professional needs to launch, manage, and build a research business. Organized into four sections, "Getting Started," "Running the Business," "Marketing," and "Researching," the book walks you through every step of the process. Author and long-time independent researcher Mary Ellen Bates covers everything from "is this right for you?" to closing the sale, managing clients, promoting your business, and tapping into powerful information sources.

"The most comprehensive manual on one of the most desired home businesses we know."

—Paul & Sarah Edwards,
authors, *Working From Home*

2003/360 pp/softbound/ISBN 0-910965-62-5 • $29.95

Choosing and Using a News Alert Service

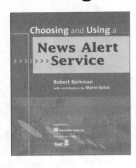

By Robert Berkman

There are dozens of competing firms that offer an e-mail based news alert service. But how to know which one is best? This comprehensive new guide explains how these tools work and then identifies, compares, and evaluates more than two dozen free, inexpensive, and fee-based alert services. It not only helps you pick the right one, but also advises how to get the most out of the news alert once you begin the service. A detailed appendix also compares specific news source coverage for the major news alert vendors.

2004/127 pp/softbound/ISBN 0-57387-224-5 • $79.95

Business Statistics on the Web
Find Them Fast—At Little or No Cost

By Paula Berinstein

Statistics are a critical component of business and marketing plans, press releases, surveys, economic analyses, presentations, proposals, and more—yet good statistics are notoriously hard to find. In this practical guide, statistics guru Paula Berinstein (author of six previous books including *Finding Statistics Online* and *The Statistical Handbook on Technology*) shows readers how to use the Net to find statistics about companies, markets, and industries, how to organize and present statistics, and how to evaluate them for reliability. Here are dozens of easy-to-use tips and techniques for manuevering around obstacles to find the statistics you need. Supported by a Web page.

2003/240 pp/softbound/ISBN 0-910965-65-X • $29.95